Embers a

Embers and Ashes

Memoirs of an Arab Intellectual

By Hisham Sharabi

Translated by Issa J. Boullata

OLIVE
BRANCH
PRESS

An imprint of Interlink Publishing Group, Inc.
www.interlinkbooks.com

First published in 2008 by

OLIVE BRANCH PRESS
An imprint of Interlink Publishing Group, Inc.
46 Crosby Street
Northampton, Massachusetts 01060
www.interlinkbooks.com

This English translation was seen by Professor Hisham Sharabi (1927–2005) of Georgetown University in Washington, DC, and benefited from his comments and from the editing of his unnamed editor.

Originally published in Arabic as *Al-Jamr wa al-Ramad: Dhikrayat Muthaqqaf 'Arabi* (Beirut: Dar al-Tali'a, 1978). Permission to translate it was gratefully received from the author and Dar al-Tali'a in Beirut.

Two excerpts from an earlier version of this English translation were published in:

Salma Khadra Jayyusi, ed. *Anthology of Modern Palestinian Literature*. New York: Columbia University Press, 1992.

Munir Akash and Khaled Mattawa, eds. *Post Gibran: New Arab American Writing*. Bethesda, MD: Jusoor, 1999.

Library of Congress Cataloging-in-Publication Data

Sharabi, Hisham, 1927–2005.
 [Jamr wa-al-ramad. English]
 Embers and ashes : memoirs of an Arab intellectual / by Hisham Sharabi ; translated from the Arabic by Issa J. Boullata.
  p. cm.
 Translation of: al-Jamr wa-al-ramad.
 Includes bibliographical references.
 ISBN 978-1-56656-702-2 (pbk.)
 1. Sharabi, Hisham, 1927-2005. 2. Palestinian Arabs—United States—Biography.
 3. Georgetown University—Biography. I. Title.
 JC273.S44A3 2005
 305.892'74073092—dc22
 [B]

                    2007025649

Printed and bound in the United States of America

To request our complete 40-page full-color catalog, please call us toll free at 1-800-238-LINK, email us at info@interlinkbooks.com, visit our website at www.interlinkbooks.com, or write to Interlink Publishing, 46 Crosby Street, Northampton, MA 01060

Contents

Preface

Early in 1974, I decided to return for good to my Arab home-land—at long last.

That summer, I left Washington, DC with my wife and two daughters. We had arranged to stay for a time in a small apartment in Ras Beirut owned by a friend of mine who was a professor at the American University of Beirut. A short while later, I borrowed a sum of money and bought a plot of land in al-Mashraf, to the south of Beirut, where my younger daughter Layla's school was located (she had just turned five). I began happily to build a small house there. It was to be our permanent residence.

At the beginning of winter, early in 1975, in plenty of time before my Lebanese visa was about to expire, I went to the Lebanese Department of Public Security to replace our visitors' visas with a residency permit for my family and me. After hours of delay and of being referred from one desk to another, my wife and I submitted the application to the officer responsible. We waited patiently for several weeks, but received no reply. We were obliged to submit a separate application to renew our visas while we waited for approval of the residency permit. We were eager, even anxious, and called at intervals for information on the status of our application. I remember that day well, a gorgeous day, early in spring. After I had waited for a long time in a hall crowded with "foreigners," the officer came to me and informed me that my application had been rejected. I asked him for the reason.

"I can tell you nothing," he replied. "Orders came from above."

I returned to my office. I was very sad. Never mind that I was editor-in-chief of the prestigious *Journal of Palestine Studies*, published in English by the Institute of Palestine Studies and Kuwait University. After all I had done for it, I was unable to obtain permission to live in this land. Was it for such disregard that I had left my secure life and permanent post and accepted an uncertain future, an unsettled life? I had returned to it in order to work for this nation, this land… Like so many intellectuals returning to serve their homeland, I was discovering that the nation and the homeland did not care for me and my dreams. Reality did not conform to my vision.

I went to my friend Dr. Munir Shamma'a and told him the depressing thing that had happened. He contacted our friend Dr. Najib Abu Haydar, a former minister of education, who immediately contacted the director of public security and asked to see him. On the next day, he obtained for me a residency permit valid for a year.

In the meantime, the architect informed us that our home in al-Mashraf would be ready by the end of the summer. Maybe things were not so bad as I had imagined. We returned to Washington at the beginning of the summer holidays to make arrangements for our final move. I planned to submit my formal resignation to Georgetown University, where I had been on the faculty since 1953.

At the end of summer, when it was time for us to return to Beirut, conditions in Lebanon had taken a turn for the worse, and we had to postpone our trip. By December 1975, the bad conditions unchanged, I decided to see the Lebanese situation for myself. I went by way of Amman, which was crowded with refugees from Beirut. Hardly a house, an apartment, or a room was left unrented. The day before I was to leave for Beirut, "Black Saturday" took place; tens of innocent civilians in Beirut were killed point blank on being identified by their ID cards as belonging to one religious group or another.

I returned to Washington like a defeated soldier. I could no longer contemplate resignation and relocation; I renewed my contract with Georgetown University. I registered my elder daughter Nadiya at the university and my younger daughter Layla at the local grade school. That was it. We had no choice but to stay in Washington—where we have remained to this day.

This book is the fruit of that unsettled period. I began writing it during the summer of 1975 in order to record in it the end of a phase of my life, a phase I thought had ended, and the beginning of a new phase, one I thought had begun or was about to begin. The new phase, however, has not yet been realized, and the previous one continues. I have a feeling at this moment that the opportunity has passed and that I will never return to my homeland, but will instead spend the rest of my life here, in this foreign country, and I will die in it. But no... That will not happen. My people are a part of my life, the part I have never abandoned, and my homeland is ever in my heart. I cannot relinquish it. I shall return, one day...

Three friends have accompanied this book since the beginning and have overwhelmed me with their sympathy and affection in its difficult moments. They are Adonis, Hasan al-Ibrahim, and Halim Barakat. To them, my permanent love.

I thank Adonis in particular because of the Arabic language corrections he made to the book without changing its style in the least, leaving it simple and unaffected as I wanted it to be.

—Hisham Sharabi
Washington, DC
May 20, 1978

—One—

-1-

We reached Lydda airport at sunset. It was a very cold day in the middle of December, 1947. The roads were empty except for British armored vehicles. Yusuf Sayigh's Humber was the only civilian car on the road between Jerusalem and Lydda. He was taking his brother Fayiz and me to the airport as we were on our way to America for higher studies; Fayiz was going to Georgetown University and I to the University of Chicago.

We had been in Jerusalem the day before, and had stayed at Claridge Hotel in Qatamun managed by Farid 'Ataya. In the afternoon, Joseph Salama and I had gone to Cinema Rex to see a movie, *Habib al-'Umr* (Sweetheart of my life), featuring Farid al-Atrash and Samiya Jamal. The theater was full and life was going on as usual, as though nothing was happening in Palestine.

In the little desolate airport, the TWA employee told us that our airplane was delayed and that departure was put off until the morning of the next day. We returned to Lydda to spend the night at a small hotel after Yusuf Sayigh said goodbye to us and returned to Jerusalem. That was my last night in Palestine.

The next morning, we boarded the airplane. From the window, I cast a last look at Jaffa, my hometown. I saw it from the sea side as we flew over the port. I could clearly see al-'Ajami neighborhood and the white Orthodox church next to our house. I thought I had a glimpse of our home on the top of al-'Araqtanji Hill…. A few moments after that, Jaffa disappeared from my view and I no longer saw anything but the long white shore behind which orange groves stretched out to the distant horizon.

-2-

I now ask myself as I write these words many years later: How was it that we left our homeland while the war was on and the Zionist Jews were preparing to seize our country?

It never occurred to me to ask that question at the time, nor did it occur to my friend Fayiz. The fact that Jews of our age, including young women, were all in military service was something that never crossed our minds, nor did the idea of postponing our studies in order to remain in our homeland and fight. There were people, we assumed, who would fight on our behalf. They were those who had fought in the 1936 rebellion and would fight again in the future. They were peasants who were not in need of specialized higher education in the West. Their natural place was here, on this land. As for us intellectuals, our place was at another level. When we fought, we fought at the front of thought. We engaged in bitter battles of the mind.

-3-

I remember clearly what was happening at the time I left home.

Toward the end of 1947, a strong wave of enthusiasm prevailed in Arab countries, occasioned by the UN resolution to partition Palestine. Students at the American University of Beirut demonstrated in the streets, asking to be enlisted as volunteers in the ranks of the Deliverance Army (*Jaysh al-Inqadh*). Their request was granted and a large number of them registered their names at volunteer centers. They were instructed to be at Martyrs' Square on the next day to be transported to Homs for military training. From the hundreds who had registered their names, only a small number reported the following day.

My friend Yusuf Ibish told me about another incident that occurred during the same period, an incident in which he and a friend of his had been involved. Yusuf was one of those whose enthusiasm had been kindled. He and his friend had decided to join the Deliverance Army, and so they went to Damascus directly, Yusuf's old and respectable family being well known there. They went straight to the office of Taha Pasha al-Hashimi, commander in chief of the Deliverance Army, and asked to meet him. After a short period of waiting, Taha Pasha received them in a kind and friendly manner, and offered them coffee. But he refused to let them join the Deliverance Army.

"Dear sons," he said, "fighting is not for young men like you. I advise you to return to your classrooms. You are sons of respectable families. You are educated and can serve your homeland by means of learning and knowledge, not by means of war and guns. There are others who are capable of carrying guns."

-4-

The strange thing was that both Fayiz and I were politically committed (we were both members of the Syrian Social Nationalist Party) and possessed a high degree of social consciousness. Yet we both left our country at a time of severe trial without any hesitation or feeling of guilt, as though the matter was a natural thing requiring no further thought. In my attempt, now, to explain that behavior, not to justify it, I find myself totally incapable. Perhaps the fact that we were educated helped to throw dust in our eyes. We had come to see things from an odd angle—the viewpoint of abstract thought. Thus, the world appeared to us as the subject of our speech and thought, not as a space for the realization of our actions. We thought it was sufficient to love our homeland with all our heart and to dream of a great future for our nation; we owed our world no other obligation than to be sincere.

-5-

When the Palestinian shore disappeared from my view, I opened the little table in front of my seat and began writing the letter every departing traveler writes—sometimes on paper, sometimes in his heart.

When we reached America, the country was having a snowstorm the likes of which had not been experienced in a long time. Snow was piling up in New York and Chicago, and all means of transportation were cut off. It seemed impossible for me to reach Chicago from Washington, where our airplane had landed at Andrews Air Force Base after midnight. Shortly afterward, however, trains resumed their normal schedules and I took the train to Chicago, after passing circuitously by way of Richmond, Roanoke, and New York. I arrived fourteen hours later, having traveled hundreds of miles through high snowbanks.

A car let me off at the entrance of International House on 59th Street, in Chicago's South Side, where the university is situated, near the shore of Lake Michigan. As soon as I got out of the car, I heard a voice saying in Arabic, "Welcome to Chicago! The city has lit up at your arrival!"

Turning to the source of the voice, I saw my friend Rashid Fakhri standing at the entrance, with a bright smile on his face. I rushed to him and embraced him with deep joy. We then entered the building, carrying my luggage. I took my room keys, and Rashid left me on the understanding that we would meet again after I had had some rest.

-6-

I entered my room and closed the door. For the first time since I had left Lydda airport, I was thinking calmly. Here I was at last in America. My dreams had come true. I had arrived at the University of Chicago, and I was now in my private room at the International House. But feelings of loneliness overtook me. My heart was about to burst, and I was about to cry. I wanted to return, I wanted to return to my homeland, to my family, to the Party that I had left behind.

A dream realized is like a desire satisfied: it leaves a dreary void behind it. At that moment I determined to return home in the shortest time possible. I would study to obtain a master's degree only, and would thus be home again within a year. I felt some comfort at the idea. It never occurred to me at the time that I would spend the greater part of my lifetime in America, nor that my first return to my Arab homeland would only be for a short and tragic period.

-7-

I woke up early the next day to the crackling sound of heating pipes turning on. I went barefoot to the window. I felt the bite of the cold but was unable to see anything outside because of the fog and the snow. I took a shower and shaved, then I went downstairs to the cafeteria for breakfast. It was empty except for a few students. After breakfast, I put on my overcoat and sat in the lounge, waiting for Rashid to come and take me to the registration office.

When we stepped outside, an icy blast hit us. I had never been so cold in my life. We walked to the university in deep snow, and I felt that my head was about to split open from icy wind.

The first thing about the university campus that drew my attention was its beautiful Gothic architectural style, then the silence that reigned over everything. The piles of snow absorbed all sounds, softening and muffling them, even the ringing of distant bells. Memory took me back to Beirut and I heard the bells of College Hall announce the start of morning classes as we hurried to our classroom.

—*Two*—

-1-

All those who studied at the American University of Beirut came from the wealthy or, at least, the middle class. From among the tens of thousands of our people's young men, we were the entitled few given the opportunity to acquire serious learning and a higher education. In spite of that, we did not feel we enjoyed special privileges denied to others. We were accustomed to living in big houses and to enjoying life as we liked. To be deprived of anything had no meaning for us; happiness was, we felt, our natural right. At a young age, we learned to regard the poor in a special way. Poverty was a part of our life, yet it was outside it, far from it, like the huts spread out around our magnificent neighborhoods. The poor were miserable human beings whom we pitied and felt compassion for, but they belonged to another world. Beggars who filled the streets of our cities were a natural sight to us. They did not disturb us, nor prick our conscience. It did not occur to us to imagine a relationship between our wealth and their misery. We used to feel pity for those wretched creatures, and that feeling of ours used to give us deep, moral comfort. Whenever we gave a beggar a small coin and he began to call upon God to grant us success and preserve our youth and keep us safe for our parents, we felt that God had already begun rewarding us for our good deed: we were satisfied with ourselves, and our virtues grew larger in our sight.

My grandmother came from a pious, aristocratic family. She used to give alms to the poor every Friday, after the noon prayer. She used to turn up the radio as loud as possible to listen to the recitation of the Holy Qur'an, and the house was filled with the voice of the reader and with the smoking incense she carried around from room to room as she uttered prayers and invocations. After the Friday sermon, the poor used to come in tens and sit in the garden in front of the eastern entrance of the house next to the kitchen. They were given food that they ate in silence, standing in the sun or sitting on the entrance steps. After that, my grandmother used to distribute old clothes and a little money to them. She also gave them a few loaves of bread—after she had "pressed" them on my head while reciting, three times, the Verse of the Throne from the Holy Qur'an. In spite of my grumbling about my grandmother's "pressing" and her mutterings, I used to accept these rituals without question. I never felt angry or embarrassed at what these acts of piety and charity represented, not until many years later, after my grandmother had died and I had begun to see life in another light.

The most important values in the life of the social class to which I belonged were social status, family name, and ostentatious generosity toward guests. Dignity had a personal meaning for members of this class, the least thing aroused their sense of dignity. Thus, during the period of foreign occupation, nationalist feeling among them took the form of dignity insulted, rather than the form of a national right or freedom trampled—as if to say that family dignity, the national right, and freedom itself were equal, even equivalent, things. That the general population lived a life of humiliation and repression, their dignity insulted every day, was a matter never even conceived of by this class. The national consciousness with which we grew up had nothing in it to connect our lives and work with the reality of our people and their life. Independence used simply to mean getting rid of the foreigners who occupied positions of authority in our country and thus deprived us from enjoying those positions ourselves. As for the liberation of a people and a society—in the sense of restoring man's humanity and society's unity and freedom—that was a matter about which we were in the dark.

As for the leaders and intellectuals of this class, in whose care our minds were formed, they used to see society and history through the prism of their class position, its values and interest. The past for them was the golden age par excellence, the age of power and glory. Contrasting the past with the present was a painful act because it highlighted the difference between greatness and ignominy. Our leaders and teachers hated the West and loved it at the same time. The West for them was the source of all that their souls desired and, at the same time, the source of their humiliation and misery. They ingrained in us an inferiority complex toward the West, as well as a complex to sanctify it. Our national idea, thus, took on a fanatical quality. Sound social and historical conceptualization was totally alien to us.

-2-

I had hardly started my college studies when the first crisis after Lebanon's independence occurred. That was in November 1943; I was a freshman. The French High Commissioner made an emotional decision, sent the Senegalese troops to Parliament, and closed Parliament by force. He then ordered that a number of leaders be arrested, including Bishara al-Khuri, president of the republic, and Riyad al-Sulh, the prime minister. He appointed Emile Idda to head a temporary government friendly to de Gaulle. There were disturbances in the country, and political parties declared a general strike. Schools closed and demonstrations broke out in many quarters, until the French finally yielded to the national demands. They then released the arrested leaders and withdrew their forces from the streets; Parliament returned to its session and raised the new Lebanese flag.

Not since the Syrian Revolt of the 1920s had there occurred so widespread a revolutionary movement by the people against French imperialism. In those days, no agents or spies at the American University of Beirut infiltrated the ranks of the students and the faculty at the behest of the president and administration of the university. Students and faculty were united in their support of the strike and their opposition to the colonizers. Demonstrations used to start in the mornings when student groups marched in all sections of Beirut, then headed toward al-Ma'rad, Martyrs' Square, and Spears Center on Phoenicia Street. The marchers used to meet squads of Lebanese Security on the way but the latter often stood aside and did not interfere with the demonstrators. We used to return to the university in the afternoon when the demonstrations had ended. We would be tired and hungry, so we rested and prepared ourselves for the next day's march. The management of West Hall used to entertain us by showing a movie every evening. They had only one movie at that time, and it was *Blood and Sand* with Rita Hayworth and Tyrone Power. We used to see this movie every evening all through the strike period. So we came to know every scene of it by heart.

That period was full of enthusiasm and patriotism. The Lebanese were all united, and they struggled for one purpose that transcended all sectarian and group interests. I remember the pictures of the armed men at Bshamun, where members of the government who were not arrested took refuge, headed by Al-Mir Majid Arslan in hunting gear, with a shotgun on his shoulder and a revolver at his waist. I also remember a secret newspaper distributed freely in the streets of Beirut, conveying news of victories everywhere. Arab students (Palestinians, Syrians, Iraqis, and Saudis) took part in the demonstrations with their Lebanese schoolmates, as though the country were theirs and the French enemy their enemy. No states, no sovereignties yet divided the Arabs. We used to feel really that Lebanon was our homeland and that we were all one nation. How happy those days were. Who could dream then that fifteen years later, in 1958, Lebanon would turn into an arena for civil war, or that in 1975 it would become a stage for massacres unparalleled in the twentieth century?

When the disturbances came to an end and the French forces withdrew from Beirut, Riyad al-Sulh paid a visit to the university. We received him like a conqueror and carried him on our shoulders to West Hall where he delivered a speech which we interrupted repeatedly with applause and cheers. That was the beginning of independence and the inception of a new era of our lives. That was my first experience with political action.

-3-

Imperialism for me was something real and palpable. I hated it as all my companions did. However, my hatred had an additional, direct dimension related to my personal experience as a Palestinian.

In the summer of 1941, the government of Free France took over Lebanon with the help of the British army. In the following year, it happened that I sent a letter to my father with one of the drivers whose cars transported passengers between Beirut, Haifa, and Jaffa. In the next letter, which I sent by mail, I asked my father whether he had received the letter I had sent with the driver. It appeared that my former letter had fallen into the hands of the censors, who then referred it to the intelligence service of the French army. I was summoned for investigations that continued for many weeks. I used to be summoned almost every week to the Public Security Bureau at al-Sana'i', where three men in civilian clothes sat at three old desks drinking coffee and smoking.

I was made to wait until they finished their coffee and conversation; then I answered the questions they had asked me in the previous week and the week before that; then I signed the papers they gave me. Investigations continued in this manner for about a year. Meanwhile, I had moved from Preparatory School to the freshman class at the American University. After the beginning of the school year and following the November crisis and the demonstrations, I was summoned again, this time to appear before the Military Court. The place to which I was summoned was in the Serai, a room on the right of the stairs opposite the Capuchin Church. I arrived half an hour before my appointment, so I sat on the stairs. When the time came, the orderly beckoned to me, and I entered a long, dark room, at one end of which stood a platform enclosed in a three-sided wooden railing. A French officer sat at the other end of it reading some papers before him. When I entered, a young Lebanese man acting as an interpreter led me to the platform. He stood aside at a distance equal to that between me and the officer. The latter continued studying the papers without raising his head or showing any sign that he was aware of my presence. I stood at the platform, one arm on the railing, one leg behind the other, as one might do standing on a balcony and watching what was happening in the street. Suddenly I heard the officer shout at me in French: "Stand straight, you dirty person [*salaud*]. Where do you think you are?"

I was startled. I stood straight as if I had been a soldier commanded to attention. My heart beat fast, and sweat dampened my forehead. I felt an awe, which soon turned to self-scorn, before this foreigner. The meeting took less than five minutes, at the end of which the officer announced I was innocent of the charge of espionage of which I had been accused. He warned me not to send letters outside Lebanon except by official mail. I went out, my head bowed and tears welling in my eyes. I was ashamed and angry that the Frenchman had insulted me.

I had not uttered a single word in response to him! What was the use of education and learning if one could be humiliated and silenced in one's own homeland?

I experienced something similar in Jaffa the following summer. During the summer holidays, I went to the C.I.D., the criminal investigations department, to obtain a permit to return to Beirut to continue my studies. I had to present a letter showing that I was a registered student there.

I took my papers to the appropriate office located on al-Mustaqim Street leading into Tel Aviv. I stood in line waiting for my turn.

"Your name?"

I gave the British officer my name.

"Why are you going to Lebanon?"

"To continue my studies."

"What kind of studies?"

"I will finish my secondary studies this year."

He took my papers and studied them a little.

"These papers are not complete," he said.

"Impossible," I answered sharply. "I've done all that the passports department asked for."

"I told you: These papers are not complete," he said in a loud voice and a commanding tone.

I tried to draw his attention to the text of the law, but he ignored me.

"Next," he called out.

I didn't know what to do. I stepped out of the line, torn by various feelings—fear, anger, and a sense of humiliation. I waited for about one hour. When the officer had given the last permit, I went to him again, politely this time, and I begged him—in a completely helpless voice—to reconsider my application. He knew he had humiliated me, so he took the papers and stamped the exit visa on my passport without uttering a word. He did not hand me back my passport, but rather threw it in my direction. I felt as outraged as if he had slapped me. I went out quietly but was about to burst with anger at him, at myself, and at the whole world. I spoke with no one all day long after that.

A similar incident involved a friend of mine. He told me about it upon my return to 'Akka (Acre), where my grandfather lived and where I used to spend the summer holidays. My friend Kamil Arna'ut used to work at the oil refinery near Haifa. He once invited a group of his American colleagues at the company to visit the archeological sites in 'Akka. After visiting the old city, they went to the citadel, which the British were using as a prison at that time. The director of the prison was a British officer married to a Jewish woman; he was known for his hatred of the Arabs. When foreign visitors came to the citadel, it was his custom to show them around and to explain its history to them himself. This officer received Kamil's American friends with open arms and accompanied them around, telling them the history of the citadel and pointing out to them its special features. As he talked, he noticed Kamil among the visitors. He stopped talking, his face turned red with anger.

"I'm not a guide for natives," he said in a voice heard by all those who were in the hall. "Leave the hall and wait outside."

When Kamil told me about that moment, I was overwhelmed by the same feelings of hatred, anger, and resentment against the foreigners who were humiliating us in our homeland—for any, or no, reason whatsoever.

-4-

The intellectual atmosphere at the American University of Beirut was that which was prevalent in the middle and upper classes, namely, the atmosphere of the "learned" and the "educated." The university had become part of this climate; by its very structure, it represented the dominant forces within these classes and served their interests and values.

It was not surprising, therefore, that we students were not expected to change much on the intellectual level. In our studies there, we learned how to connect causes with results, and we formed a general idea of the "scientific method." But all our education was not sufficient to make a radical change in our mentality, in the way we thought. I am reminded of the first "scientific" experiences I had in my secondary studies and of Mr. As'ad, who used to conduct various experiments in front of us so that we might see for ourselves how it was possible to appreciate theories in the light of scientific proofs. He used to pour colored liquid in a test tube, heat it over a flame until it boiled, and let us see how its color changed. He would then pour it into another test tube, and its color would change again. Sometimes he made a mistake in the process and, when the last stage was reached and a certain result was expected, the expected did not happen. Something else would happen instead: the color of the liquid would not change, or the test tube would explode, and the students would burst out laughing.

Those were the results we loved most. But we always returned to other scientific attempts, expecting that a test tube would explode or an apparatus would be burnt so that we might find respite from the sheer boredom that prevailed in our studies of "experimental science."

As a means of analysis, scientific method was easy to grasp. Indeed many of those who studied physics, chemistry, pharmacy, and medicine at the American University of Beirut did grasp it. As for us who specialized in the humanities and the social sciences, understanding—in the sense of being able to recognize syntheses and to relate concepts to historical and social reality—was an extremely difficult problem. I suffered the consequences of this problem immediately upon joining the University of Chicago, for I discovered that I was unable to understand the thoughts I was exposed to in the lectures and discussions. Language was not the cause, for my English was good, and I spoke and wrote it fluently. What added to my confusion at Chicago was that most of the lectures and courses that I had chosen for the first semester had to do with subjects I thought I was very familiar with, having studied most of them at the American University of Beirut.

At the American University, the freedom we exercised was much less than most people used to believe. Our life as students at the university was subject to two authorities we had no power to contest: the authority of the administration and the authority of the professor. The administration's authority over us was analogous to the state's authority over its citizen: it was comprehensive and complete, and we did not know where it began and where it ended. As for the professor's authority, it was like a father's authority over his children: it was imposed from on high and did not countenance opposition or contradiction.

I do not recall a single professor of mine at the university who admitted, even once, that he was in error, or who confessed ignorance or expressed doubt and refrained from taking a decisive position, preferring to reconsider a thought and reflect further on it. All my professors maintained images of themselves as reliable sources unaffected by the shadows of doubt. They entered the classroom with the confidence of officers entering the barracks. Their authority there was absolute, and their word, final. They believed that our good behavior meant acceptance of their authority and submission to it, and that our silence was a sign of appreciation for the lectures they improvised as they walked up and down, their eyes staring at the ceiling rapt, in deep thought.

The professoriate, almost without exception, followed the same style in their lectures: a style of description, oratory, and preaching. They looked at matters from their own points of view and were not embarrassed to offer their personal opinions as if they were solid, objective truths. If we asked them questions that implied some criticism or placed them in difficult situations, they took defensive positions and answered our questions in a hostile spirit, making us withdraw from a confrontation into silence.

I do not remember that a single one of our Arab professors ever aimed in his lectures at helping us understand, much less achieve, independent thinking (with the possible exception of Charles Issawi). Their main obsession was to present themselves as authority figures and to strengthen or justify their own points of view. They took any disagreement with their viewpoint as a personal insult, so we learned not to dispute them and to accept submissively what they said.

The purpose of the process of our education at the university, as in the family and at school, was basically to render us obedient and to subjugate us psychologically to a patriarchal ethos. No wonder, therefore, that our critical and analytical abilities remained weak (as I discovered in Chicago) while the tendency to submit to the opinions of those reputedly more knowledgeable than ourselves was conditioned and reinforced—namely, the professors and doctors whose ranks we dreamed of joining one day.

Another result of our university education was that we learned to submit to the authority of the printed word, just as we submitted to the heard word. We became intellectually paralyzed in relation to what we read, especially if it was of foreign origin, and we became accustomed to paying scant attention to its meaning and the content, concentrating instead on the effect and the impressions the words made. Emotion, not reason, was the strongest factor in what we grasped and deemed proper and correct. We were accustomed to superficial, fast reading, and poetry—for many of us—was the favorite reading matter.

-5-

In the fall of 1970, I was invited to spend the academic year as a visiting professor at the American University of Beirut. At the beginning of that year, a symposium was held at al-Bustan Hotel in Bayt Miri. It was sponsored by the Ford Foundation and a number of professors from the university participated, including Dr. Charles Malik, Dr. Qustantin Zurayq, my friend Ibrahim Ibrahim, and the president of the university at the time, Dr. Samuel Kirkwood. I mention this symposium because it reminded, and still reminds me, of the intellectual atmosphere that prevailed at the university during my school days, especially regarding Dr. Charles Malik, who had remained unchanged all those decades later.

Dr. Malik played exactly the same role in the symposium as he had in our school days. After the opening of the symposium and as we sat around a large round table, Dr. Malik gave a long lecture in the same manner and tone that he had used to lecture in to us in the classroom. After the lecture, we opened a period of discussion and questions. Hardly had a person begun to speak, to ask a question, when Malik would interrupt him, offering a long response of his own, thus effectively silencing him and preventing him or anyone else from exchanging ideas.

I did not keep silent as I used to do when I was a student. I stood up and said to him that the frame of reference that he assumed in his lecture lacked clarity, and I pointed out the historical and social factors that should be taken into consideration. In the course of my comment, I used the expression "post-Christian era," meaning the industrial period in Europe, during which Church dominion over European society ceased and the prevailing ideology became secular and not religious.

Malik responded to my comment angrily, "What you have said does not deserve to be commented on. This expression is a stupid, journalistic one that you picked up from *Time* or a similar magazine."

Listening to him, I remembered the kinds of arrogance and the styles of intellectual sarcasm to which he had subjected us during our years of study at the university. He no longer frightened me; rather, he bored me. His words and his thoughts were purely defensive and aimed at imposing himself on his listeners. Merleau-Ponty's statement on those who speak "in the name of truth and high values" came to mind: "In the person who always speaks of high values, ethics, and man's inner self, there lurks a secret tendency to violence, hatred, and fanaticism."

I will never forget a small incident that happened in that same year, small in itself but extremely important because of its significance. My office was in Bliss Hall, opposite his. One day he came to me and said he would like to talk to me about an important matter. So I went into his office. He closed the door behind me, asked me to sit on a chair in front of his, and said:

"I've heard that *Al-Sayyad* magazine says you're a Marxist. Is this true?" He then continued, "I'm concerned about you. We have to speak frankly on this subject. Marxism is something unreasonable. I don't believe it is possible that you've taken this road."

Until that time, and for many years, I had convinced myself that it was possible to keep my old friends in spite of my intellectual differences with them. I used to be pleased with myself because most of my university friends were still my friends. I was pleased that time and life's experiences had not broken the bonds that held us together. Yet at that moment, I realized that friendships wither and die but we refuse to admit the fact; we pretend they are still alive, and we carry them in our hearts as lifeless corpses.

I was not so much disturbed by his question as hurt by the contempt implicit in the paternalistic and condescending manner in which he was raising the matter with me. I believed that our collegial relationship was based on equality and mutual respect, but it became clear to me immediately that our relationship even that day was one-sided. For him it was still based on subjugation and domination on his part, his expectation being submission and dependence on my part.

Strangely, it never occurred to me to ask him why his thought tended to be metaphysical, or to say to him, "Your ideology is reactionary, and it is better for you to abandon it."

From that time on, however, the old bond which held me to Charles Malik was broken, and it was no longer possible for me to justify much of a continuing relationship with him.

-6-

Classes at the American University of Beirut were taught in English. Some of our professors spoke English fluently, such as Charles Issawi. Others spoke it with some difficulty. Most of them used to come to the classroom essentially unprepared. Any thoughts or opinions they had on the subject of that day's lesson they delivered in an improvised manner.

Dr. Charles Malik's teaching style was distinguished from that of others in some ways. It was his custom to start the lesson by asking one of the students to read a certain passage from the text assigned for that day. Barely would the student have begun to read a few lines when Dr. Malik would interrupt him and ask him to explain what he had just read. If the student failed to respond quickly, Dr. Malik would ask another student, then a third and a fourth until he had made all the members of the class feel they did not know the right answer and should be convinced of their complete ignorance. At that moment, Dr. Malik would begin addressing the question to which nobody but he had the answer. He might then move to another subject, but always in the same manner. His lectures, though improvised, were actually enjoyable and were attended by many students and visitors. The students used to fear Dr. Malik on account of the depth of his thoughts and the difficulty of understanding them, a fact that strengthened his intellectual reputation over the years.

-7-

When I joined the University of Chicago, I discovered that there were English expressions whose meanings I understood but that I seldom used such as: *probably, somewhat, to some extent.* These expressions are used to lessen the absolute certainty or decisiveness of a statement and to lend it a measure of moderation and poise. Yet our professors at the American University of Beirut rarely used expressions of that sort in their lectures. I became aware of the phenomenon, in fact, only several weeks after I arrived at the University of Chicago. I noticed that my professors and classmates there never spoke without using modifiers. I also noticed that whenever I took part in a conversation I used decisive and categorical expressions of absoluteness and finality. I soon discovered that the reason was not language alone and that thought and style of expression had something to do with it. An idea to my mind had to be either right or wrong. If it was right, I felt I had to defend it fully. It was so perhaps because we believed, like our fathers and professors, that we were always right and that others were always wrong. Most of the time, my position was defensive and I rejected all kinds of criticism. After some time, I noticed that my American classmates began to find this behavior of mine strange, especially my tenacious clinging to my point of view. They refrained from entering into discussions with me.

In discussions I was like one playing a zero-sum game that ends only in one side winning totally and another losing utterly; that is, it ends with a victor and a vanquished.

I will never forget the afternoon I spoke with my professor, Charles Morris, under the shade of a tree in the university court-yard, about the lecture he had given in the morning of that day.

"Anyway, truth will inevitably impose itself," I said to him.

Morris was silent for a moment, then he said calmly: "Forget about the truth. It is not our problem now."

I was shocked by his words. Truth to me was a sacred thing and the object of all search. I did not come to understand what Morris meant until a long time afterward when truth manifested itself to me in its reality: it was just an intellectual concept among other intellectual concepts. From that moment, I began to see matters in a new light, one that differed completely from what I had been accustomed to until then. But it was a long time before the process was complete.

Our professors at the American University of Beirut were not interested in scholarly research and publication. I do not remember that any of them ever published a book of any value. Their intellectual laziness used to be reflected in the treatment of the subjects on which we wrote papers that we submitted to them for various courses of study. I can truthfully say that, during my years at the university, not a single one of my professors ever guided me with regard to the correct method of research. Nor did I receive any criticism or analysis of a paper submitted to any of them. When I graduated from the university, I hardly knew the meaning of *methodology* or *research* in any real sense. Sources and references to me were all on a level, equally orthodox for my purposes, and

I did not know how to distinguish among them or how to evaluate them. Our professors often did not read our papers and as often returned them to us without a single remark.

Their negligence reinforced our laziness and justified it. Imitating our professors, on the other hand, strengthened our penchant for literary composition and our hatred of numbers and statistics. Our feeling grew that the quantitative element in research was secondary and that sound thought was only the thought supported by strong common sense and distinguished language, rather than by the power of critical inquiry and analysis. No wonder we ended up disdaining the method prevalent in the social sciences and based on statistics and quantitative evaluation. The orientation we received led us away from adopting and respecting accurate scientific terms.

I discovered my ignorance a few weeks after I enrolled at the University of Chicago. I found that I did not understand the meaning of such basic terms as *concept*, *hypothesis*, *theory*, or *critique*, and that I could not use them correctly in my speech and writing. When I became professor of European thought at Georgetown University many years afterward, I found that Arab students (many of them were graduates of the American University of Beirut) suffered from the same problem. The word *concept* to an Arab student, for example, meant merely "idea," as it is said to mean in *Al-Mawrid* English-Arabic dictionary (and as it used to mean to me). There was no difference between that word and words like *idea*, *notion*, *thought*: they were all synonyms. It was difficult for them, as it used to be for me, to understand the distinction between *hypothesis* and *theory* and to comprehend the relation between them. The term *critique* meant to them one thing only: it meant *criticism* or *faultfinding* as it used to mean to me. This was my intellectual condition when I entered the University of Chicago, after graduating with a Bachelor of Arts degree in philosophy from the American University of Beirut.

No doubt, the personality and style of my professors had had a great effect on the development of the manner of my thinking and on my mental habits, acquired during those days and persisting for a long time afterward. When a professor treated an idea with sarcasm or belittled a certain thinker, he killed the idea and its author. So we thought. The most lethal intellectual weapon in the hands of our professors was sarcasm, and they did not hesitate to use it whatever the occasion. How easy it was for a professor to destroy all in the classroom who disagreed with his beliefs and feelings. All my professors at the American University of Beirut practiced the style of sarcasm and mockery—it didn't matter what subjects they taught. Some of them practiced sarcasm in a direct and obvious way, others in an indirect and subtle manner. I do not bear any of them any grudge, for I myself adopted the same style inadvertently when I became a professor. I now know that the motive for this practice is mostly an unconscious one, its main impetus being fear or lack of self-confidence.

-8-

In those days, each of us thought he was the wonder of his age who was more intelligent than everybody else. We were very anxious to finish our studies and begin a life full of adventures and great deeds. Only after many years of ignorance and self-delusion did I discover my error and realize that I was not a wonder of my age.

Now, after wasting many valuable years of my life, I have come to realize—unregretfully—that I am not a genius or a wonder, but rather a human being like everybody else, and that I am not different from my colleagues in intelligence nor in perspicacity. I am indeed content to be as I am, able at least to run my own life and overcome the bad effects of the coercion and the distortion to which I was subjected in my young age. Though I do not blame anybody for the lack of a genius that I believed myself once to have possessed, I cannot help asking whether my life and personality would have been what they are today if my professors and those who had a share in educating me had been less coercive in their treatment of me and less afraid for their positions, their livelihood, and their social status.

I may forgive those to whom I owe my education for their ignorance and their foolishness. But it is far more difficult to forgive them their arrogance and the moral cruelty they practiced in distorting me and calling it an education.

-9-

The overwhelming tendency of my life during my university studies was philosophism. In those days I was not able to distinguish
between philosophy and philosophism. At the philosophy department we were all philosophists—professors as well as students. I
was naturally inclined to philosophize things, that is, to see them
through veils of contemplation and thought, and not in a direct
and spontaneous manner. Perhaps that is why life used to seem so
obscure and disturbed to me, for I was unable to take it and enjoy
it in a simple and merry way as most of my colleagues did. Every
day that passed in my life was complicated and full of riddles and
psychologically painful events. Doubtlessly, the kind of thought
to which I was exposed at the American University of Beirut
strengthened my alienation from myself and increased the distance
between me and the reality of life, which I yearned to understand
and grasp.

Socrates said: "The beginning of knowledge is knowledge of
oneself." This was exactly what we, students of philosophy,
thought we had gone a long way in achieving. It did not occur to
us that what we believed to be self-knowledge was only mere delu-
sions and imaginings not at all related to reality.

We used to see this reality and express ourselves about it in
idealist abstractions derived from Descartes, Hegel, Kierkegaard,
and other philosophers. The dualism of Descartes, for example,
permitted us to place the mind above the body; the idealism of
Hegel, to bestow final value on reason; and the subjectivism of
Kierkegaard, to root reality in the "inwardness" of individual
being. (I read the following sentence yesterday in a book by
Norman Brown entitled *Life and Death* which I would have
deemed silly and thrown away if I had read it in those days: "What
the child knows consciously, the adult unconsciously, is that we are
nothing but body.")

In the religious idealist frame of mind adopted by Malik and
our other professors, there was no room for another manner of
thinking. I never heard the name of Karl Marx mentioned even
once during all the years of my study at the American University
of Beirut, nor did I ever read one word by Sigmund Freud. If we
had read Marx, we surely would have recognized that he fully

contradicted all that we were learning and believed in; how could a person think that man was not mere spirit or reason or inner being, but rather a social existent defined by a specific material reality and a specific perceptible history? And if we had read Freud, we would have discovered that what motivated man and directed his behavior and thinking were not the values and high ideals that our professors talked about and preached, but rather inner forces and motives that were ingrained in the psyche and used the conscious mind as one of their means.

In that period I used to feel what every young man felt: hunger for knowledge accompanied by yearning for prominence and thirst for excellence. My choice of philosophy as a subject of study was a result of my persistent desire to get rid of the state of psychological anxiety and intellectual disarray I was in. In the diaries I had begun to write in that period, I find the following entry for November 15, 1944: "I am trying to achieve two things: to understand my inner self through psychology and to use my reason in an organized fashion."

I find this statement strange. I do not remember that I was interested in psychology in those days, nor do I remember reading a single book on the subject—I wish I had. I believed, rather, that the best way to arrive at intellectual clarity and real knowledge of things was to study logic, not psychology. The first book I read in logic was by Jacques Maritain. Reading it took a lot of my time and strenuous effort, but I persevered in spite of the boredom and sleepiness that invaded me as I plowed through it. Notwithstanding my exertions, I benefited nothing from it. Then I happened upon a book by John Dewey entitled *The Quest for Certainty*. The title appealed to me, for that was exactly what I was seeking. But I found it boring also, although not as difficult as Maritain's book. What aroused my distaste for Dewey was his strictly pragmatic style, so I put the book away before I had finished reading it.

I developed an aversion to the books imposed on us as part of the required reading for our courses. I could not go back to some of those books until many years later, and they included Shakespeare's famous play *Macbeth*, Machiavelli's *The Prince*, and Plato's *Republic*.

-10-

What our professors liked most was for us to ask questions on the topics they were speaking about. We used to submit to their ideas and repress whatever we thought contradicted them. We used to boast to our friends by frequently mentioning the names of the philosophers whom our professors mentioned in the classroom. We used to speak about those philosophers and their books without having really read them. In my junior and senior years, the two philosophers who were favorites of mine were Kierkegaard and Berdyaev. When we graduated, we considered ourselves to be existentialist followers of the idealist religious Kierkegaardian school.

-11-

In 1945, Dr. Malik left us to become minister plenipotentiary of Lebanon in Washington. We gave him a farewell party in West Hall at which a number of students and professors spoke. They all said words to the effect that he was Plato going to America to realize his philosophy, and that it was our loss and America's gain. It never occurred to us that what Malik would do in the United States was to specialize in attacking communism, praising Christianity, and supporting the Cold War, and that he would return to Lebanon to become the ideologue of the fanatic Christian Right.

In my junior and senior years, we did not read a single philosopher in full, as far as I remember. We listened to lectures on Aristotle, Descartes, or Locke; then we thumbed through *Ethics*, *Politics*, *Meditations*, or *Two Treatises on Civil Government*, and we took down some notes—and that was the end of that. (By contrast, I took two reading courses during my first semester in the philosophy department at the University of Chicago: one dealt with Aristotle's *Politics* and the other with Hobbes's *Leviathan*. Only then, and for the first time, did I learn how a philosophical text should be read.)

In fact, we used to experience great difficulty in sitting alone and reading what was assigned to us. At any rate, there was nothing that induced us to read: the atmosphere in the study room was boring, and it was more enticing to sit at Faysal Restaurant or the Milk Bar to chat. Thus, we did not do much serious reading unless it was something each of us wanted to read on his own. Most of those who graduated from the university do not read and do not know how to read properly.

Nevertheless, we loved books very much. We carried them under our arms wherever we went and bought them at exorbitant prices. Each of us had a private library that was a physical expression of his status as an intellectual. The more books one owned, the more value he had as an intellectual in his opinion and that of others.

At the end of my studies at the university, I came to have a library containing hundreds of books I had collected book by book, having paid the price of each by depriving myself of many pleasures. My library contained most of the classics from Homer to Nietzsche, the majority being imprints of the British Everyman's Library and Random House, the American publisher. Possessing the books for us was more important than reading them: it was an end in itself. I always promised myself that I would read the books I bought as soon as the next summer holidays began. Among the books which I in fact read and that influenced me were the works of Nietzsche collected in one volume containing *Thus Spake Zarathustra, Ecce Homo, Beyond Good and Evil*, and *The Spirit of Music*. Nietzsche's ideas and philosophic style left an indelible effect on my soul. I also read two novels by Dostoevsky: *Crime and Punishment* and *The Brothers Karamazov*. After them I read Herman Melville's *Moby-Dick* and Voltaire's *Candide*. Among my unsuccessful attempts at reading stood *Paradise Lost* and *The Aeneid*. But I succeeded to some extent in enjoying *Faust* (Part One) and *Conversations with Eckermann*.

These readings and others I deemed to be on the level of high culture. For entertainment, I took Somerset Maugham, Aldous Huxley, Ernest Hemingway, Evelyn Waugh, and Graham Greene. It is strange that I stopped reading Arabic books after my freshman year. Somerset Maugham's *Of Human Bondage* and *The Moon and Sixpence* I read for the first time when I was sick during that year, and I can still feel today the freshman's pleasure I felt in reading them.

I dutifully read Huxley's famous book *Brave New World,* and I did not like it very much; then I read his great novel *Point Counter Point*, and as a result I read everything he wrote without exception after that. I did the same thing with the fiction of Hemingway, Waugh, and Greene.

After the death of Hemingway, Huxley, and Waugh in the 1960s, I completely stopped reading them. I felt that the part of my life that was connected to them through their writing had ended and that the rapport that I had with them was over. I preferred to forget as one does when a dear friend dies.

We philosophy majors constituted the distinguished elite of the university—at least in our own view. We thought we were workers in the field of thought and philosophy, while others were immersed in trivial material concerns like economics, engineering, and chemistry. We affected seriousness unintentionally and raised our voices during our philosophical discussions at the Milk Bar. We were flattered when other students gathered around our table to listen to our discussions, and when they tried to participate in them we ignored them scornfully. We purposely did not take part in athletics in order to draw attention to our occupation with matters of the spirit. Only rarely did we attend football games in which the university team played, though all university students generally went to them. We preferred to frequent cafés and movie theaters, and we went on long walks during which we spoke on philosophic topics. While our friends learned to drink alcoholic drinks, to play poker, and stay up late at the Kit Kat and the Lido nightclubs, and while they sought sex in the brothels, we were content with philosophic and literary conversations. When our friends sat with us, they purposely raised the topic of sex and told dirty stories. Our sessions would then be transformed into verbal wrangles that ended with the withdrawal of the intellectual elite in disgust and anger.

-12-

After Dr. Malik left, Kenneth Cragg became chairman of the philosophy department. In addition to being a professor of philosophy, he was an Anglican clergyman. Cragg was a meek man who said little except in the classroom. All through class time, he spoke incessantly and gave nobody an opportunity to say a word. He came to the classroom in his old clothes and with his thick glasses on. He would sit at the table, open a large, black-covered notebook, and read to us in a fluent manner until the end of the period.

He used to organize and prepare his lectures meticulously, in contrast to other professors. The number of students in his class was usually no more than four: Fu'ad Najjar, Labib Zuwiyya, Zahida al-Basha, and I; and yet he delivered his lectures to us as though he were addressing a big crowd.

Fu'ad and I went to him one day in order to talk to him "in depth" about certain subjects that we considered to be of principal importance in our lives. We said to him that we wanted to get out of the state of puzzlement and disarray in which we were and desired to arrive at certainty, religious certainty. We warmly requested him to lead us in the path of faith, for faith was the prevailing mode at the philosophy department since the days of Dr. Malik. It was necessary, we thought, for a student of philosophy to acknowledge the necessity of faith. Later I discovered that it was also necessary for the student to experience love so that he might combine the religious experience of Berdyaev and the love experience of Kierkegaard in his relationship with Regine Olsen. Cragg was embarrassed and spoke hesitantly (Fu'ad was a Druze and I a Sunni Muslim). He said that the matter was rather difficult and complicated, that its resolution was up to us, and that he could not help us. We left him feeling as though cold water had been poured on us, torn between feelings of shame and confusion.

I wrote a paper on aesthetics for Professor Cragg and I remember the opening sentence of that paper, which said, "That truth is absolute needs no argument." Cragg wrote a remark on it in red pencil, "This is wrong. Truth is not absolute or universal. There are different viewpoints regarding its essence." I was aghast, but I began to reconsider "absolute" truth without abandoning the search for it. Then, gradually, I began to move away from the theological atmosphere that dominated the philosophy department.

I was more able than Fu'ad and less able than Labib to tolerate the boredom of that philosophy class. I eventually achieved the minimum academic requirements, but Fu'ad was unable to do so. He stopped preparing himself for the examinations and stopped attending the lectures. When he did attend, he sat silently and looked at the lecturer with a smile of sorts on his lips. The professor thought he was following the lecture with interest. On the other hand, Labib wrote down every word the professor said and reproduced it on the examination.

At the end of our senior year, Fu'ad could not answer the examination questions. He sat looking at the examination book, unable to write a single word in it. He got up and handed in an empty book. Fu'ad managed to graduate with us, but he was not permitted to continue his studies there beyond the bachelor's degree. He left for Saudi Arabia a few months after I had gone to America. A few years later, he got married, had three children, and was very happy. When he died in an airplane accident in Dhahran in 1964, I lost the dearest friend I had had so far in my life.

-13-

A Lebanese young man by the name of Joseph Salama was my roommate at Bliss Hall. He had red hair, which made him appear strange to me, and so we rarely spoke to each other. In the middle of the year, Joseph left the university, having failed certain courses, and I did not see him again until the following year. During the years after that, I saw him a few times only. Then toward the end of the fourth and last year, our relations grew stronger, and we became good friends.

Joseph played an important role in my life for some time, especially when he entered the University of Chicago after the death of Antun Sa'adah. We lived together in an apartment near the University of Chicago. He did not finish his studies there, for he married an American girl, then moved with her to New York.

I, on the other hand, was to remain in Chicago until the summer of 1951 when I finished my doctoral coursework and qualifying exams and had only to write my thesis. I then moved to New York and lived with Usama Qadri, Fu'ad's friend and mine since Preparatory School. Usama had been appointed to serve as a consul of Iraq in the United States. I began writing my dissertation and working at the United Nations at the same time, remaining in New York until the beginning of 1953, when Georgetown University offered me a teaching post. I moved from New York to Washington, DC, in February of 1953. A few years later, in 1956, Joseph Salama enrolled at Georgetown University. He divorced his wife and devoted himself completely to his studies for four years. He wrote a dissertation and obtained his Ph.D. in 1960. After a disagreement in that year, our friendship came to an end as suddenly as it had started. But all of that was in the future.

At the beginning of sophomore year, I moved from Bliss Hall to the Lodge, an old house that stood in a field near the Corniche. Today the Faculty of Agriculture stands in its place. In 1944, after some repairs, the Lodge was ready to receive sixteen or seventeen students and a supervising professor (Majid Fakhri). Our house was equipped with an independent kitchen—in which to warm up the food carried to us daily from the principal cafeteria and to prepare breakfast. A young man whose name I don't remember used to serve us; his main duties were to prepare breakfast and to heat the water for our baths.

Life at the Lodge was full of cultural and artistic activities. We used to invite a professor, once a week, to take supper with us and then give a lecture afterward. The professor who sponsored the Lodge, who was someone other than the supervising professor, often participated with his wife in the evenings. They lived in a large house on the other side of the football field. They took part enthusiastically in our intellectual conversations, which dealt in particular with music, literature, and art, but I do not remember the subjects discussed because they were trivial. We used to pay a lot of money to buy magazines and expensive books for the Lodge library specializing in music, as a visible proof of our high culture.

At the Lodge, we enjoyed special privileges, the most important and pleasant of which were the evening dancing parties because they would make our friends living elsewhere jealous. Once or twice every semester, we threw these parties and invited our female friends at the university, who, for the most part, lived at the hostel on 'Abd al-'Aziz Street. We actually held the parties not at the Lodge itself but at the home of the sponsoring professor, who, together with his wife, acted as chaperones. We were not permitted to serve alcoholic drinks; most of us did not like drinking anyway. The girls would sit with the hostess and talk with her as they drank their tea, while we would spread out in other parts of the room pretending not to care. We would laugh once in a while in order to conceal our embarrassment. When a tango was played on the hand-wound gramophone, we would slowly and hesitantly go to the girls in order to ask them to dance with us. We would put our arms gingerly and loosely around their waists, and we would dance in silence to the end of the record. Then we would return to our standing places in the room, waiting for the next record while our eyes searched for the girl we wanted to dance with next. The party would soon end, at ten o'clock or eleven at the latest, and we would escort the girls to the hostel and return to the Lodge talking about what had happened at the party.

Other privileges we enjoyed at the Lodge included the large measure of freedom and the practice of self-government. We had a special regulation according to which we elected an executive committee and a chairman. The most important prerogative of the chairman was to give written permits to allow their bearer to stay outside the university after the gates were closed at 10PM. When I was elected chairman in my senior year, I used to carry the book of permits in my pocket, and whenever we happened to be outside the University after 10PM, I used to write the required permit for my friends and me, and we returned at whatever hour we chose.

Perhaps the most beautiful of my experiences at the Lodge were the friendships that developed between me and a number of those who lived in it. I remember Gaby Nasr, who lived in the room next to mine. I did not see him for a long time after 1947, but I met him in San Francisco in 1970 by coincidence. That was at Mills College, a small college for women in Oakland, near San Francisco, where I was invited to participate in a dialogue with a Jewish-American professor from Stanford University about the Palestine problem. In the question and answer period, I saw a tall and husky man raise his hand to ask the Jewish professor a question. The Jewish professor tried to give an evasive answer, but the man challenged him and the audience applauded. After the meeting, a group of students gathered around me, and among the faces surrounding me, I saw that of the husky man. He came toward me with a smile that I remembered in a flash—Gaby Nasr. We hugged each other warmly; I asked him about his circumstances and he asked me about mine. We then went together, accompanied by about twenty people, to one of the bars in Berkeley, where we continued to talk and drink beer until after midnight.

I also remember Philip Nasr-Allah. It was from him that I heard for the first time Marx's famous saying: "From each according to his ability, and to each according to his need." But Philip did not mention the source of this saying, the *Communist Manifesto,* nor did he speak to me about socialism. I don't know why not. All that he said appealed to me, but I forgot it in a short time.

My roommate was a young Iraqi man who studied economics and whose name was Muhsin Mahdi. He used to hate economics and love philosophy. He always participated in our philosophical discussions at the department and, in time, became like one of its members. He came to the University of Chicago about six months after I did, and I received him on his arrival in the summer of 1948. In Chicago he changed the subject of his specialization and wrote his thesis on Ibn Khaldun. After his graduation, he returned to Baghdad, where he was appointed as a professor at the Baghdad University. He resigned soon thereafter and returned to Chicago, where he was appointed as a professor at the Oriental Institute and, a few years later, became its director. At the beginning of the 1970s, Harvard University invited him to succeed Sir Hamilton Gibb as chairman of the department of Middle East studies and professor of Arabic. He accepted the position and moved to Harvard, where he remains.

-14-

Two young men lived in the room next to ours; one of them was a Syrian named Yahya Homsi and the other was an American named Tom Shea. Yahya was a lazy student who rarely attended lectures, especially in the morning. But he was fascinated by read-ing and had a large library that filled his little bedroom. He used to read while smoking one cigarette after another.

Whenever he went downtown in the weekend, he returned with a load of new books. He also bought books on weekdays from Khayyat's Bookshop opposite the university main gate on Bliss Avenue.

Yahya was in the habit of never finishing either reading a book or smoking a cigarette. He would forget the cigarette held between his lips until it burnt them. He would also read the first pages of a book, stopping now and then to declare that it was the greatest book he had ever read in his life. A few moments later, he would put it aside. One of Yahya's famous books was that of e.e. cummings, *The Enormous Room*, which he carried under his arm for days and spoke enthusiastically about to everyone he met, until he bought a new tome one day entitled *Le zéro et l'infini* by a writer whose name we had not yet heard of, namely, Arthur Koestler, the ex-Communist writer whose book caused a big row in Europe and the United States after the end of the Second World War. At the Lodge we were known in part by the books we advocated.

-15-

Our circle of friends included three persons not living at the Lodge, in addition to Muhsin, Tom, and Yahya. We used to meet them daily at Faysal's or at the Milk Bar. They were Hugo Lemming, a young American man who taught English at the Preparatory School; Jamko Hang Singh, a young Indian man who studied medicine at the University Hospital and now lives in Dar al-Salam; and Usama Qadri, whose father, Tahsin Qadri, was the consul of Iraq in Beirut at that time. Usama was, and still is, the closest of my friends, but I have not seen him in about ten years.

The two Americans, Tom Shea and Hugo Lemming, were particularly interested in psychology. They often discussed subjects we knew nothing about, such as the Oedipus complex and Freud's theories on sex and the interpretation of dreams. We used to scoff at those theories and make fun of them. I did not know at that time why they were interested in Freud's theories. Later on I discovered that they both hated their fathers and believed themselves to be victims of their bad treatment. Each was an only child. When I arrived in the United States, I visited their families. I first visited Lemming's family in Richmond and met his mother (I don't know whether his father was dead or had left his mother). Then I visited Tom's parents in Roanoke, which is not far from Richmond. I spent two full days with them but noticed nothing strange about the two families. However, at that time I had not come to see things clearly.

As undergraduates, we used to sit at the Milk Bar for hours on end, smoking cigarettes and drinking coffee and talking continuously. We always returned to serious topics, i.e., philosophical, literary, and political topics. I did not know then that Lemming was a leftist, and did not discover this about him until many years later.

We began to frequent a Russian bar called Nuits Blanches, situated in Hawuz al-Sa'atiyya near the tramway line. At the Nuits

Blanches, I learned to drink vodka. At first I did not like its taste, and I vomited after drinking it. I had drunk three or four glasses of it, became dizzy, and felt a sharp pain in my stomach. When I returned to the Lodge, I tried to vomit but couldn't. So Tom took me to the football field nearby where we began to walk and walk until I vomited and felt comfortable again. I refrained from drinking for a long while after that, but Tom's and Lemming's insistence made me return to drinking a glass or two whenever we went to the Nuits Blanches, and my ability to hold the liquor became better. Tom and Lemming had a powerful influence on me, regarding not only vodka, but also many other things. They were the first foreigners of my age group I was acquainted with who rebelled against their families and their milieu and began searching for a new life that they could shape as they wanted. I especially admired their freedom and their ability to live their private lives without any inhibitions. There was no subject that was forbidden to speak about as far as they were concerned. And perhaps what I admired most about them was their permanent thirst for every kind of new experience.

Once, Tom and Muhsin were visiting Lemming in his room in Sage Hall, and they began speaking about hypnotism. Tom suggested that Lemming try to hypnotize him. On doing so, Tom fell into a deep sleep immediately, perhaps because he was psychologically ready to be hypnotized. However, when Lemming and Muhsin tried to awaken him, they could not and so they decided to bring him back to the Lodge unconscious. He sleepwalked with them, oblivious to everything. In his room, they tried to awaken him again but couldn't. They were afraid and were about to take him to the hospital, had he not tripped and fallen. He woke suddenly and began asking, "Where am I? Where am I?" That was the last time Lemming tried hypnotism in our group.

Another incident occurred which might have had more serious consequences than it did. Tom and Lemming decided one day to try smoking hashish. They knew how conservative the other members of the group were, so they did not mention their project to anyone. One evening, they took the tramway to Martyrs' Square and went to a café in the market that one of the University servants had told them about. According to Tom's story (which he told me in Washington in 1958—that is, twelve years later), they entered the café and were met by a man who appeared to be the owner.

They told him in broken Arabic that they wanted to smoke hashish. He motioned to them to follow him and went down a dark stairway before them. He opened a door under which there was a chink of light and gestured to them to enter. They entered a hall in which there were some tables at which men sat silently smoking their waterpipes. Tom and Lemming sat at one table, and a man brought them two cups of tea and one waterpipe. Tom and Lemming smoked the waterpipe in turn and drank tea until all the tobacco was gone. A moment later Lemming said, "I have a headache, let's get out of this place."

The hashish had affected him adversely, for instead of feeling high and relaxed, he felt depressed and spiteful. They walked in silence until they reached Martyrs' Square, just in front of the police station. It was past two o'clock in the morning. They stood under a streetlight and Lemming asked Tom to leave him alone and walk away. He explained that he wanted to pass the rest of the evening by himself. Tom tried to convince him that he should return to the university and he began to insist. Lemming suddenly picked up a big stone from the ground and screamed in Tom's face saying, "I'll break your head if you won't leave me alone." And he meant what he said.

Tom pretended to acquiesce and walked away in the direction of Ras Beirut. A few steps away, he hid inside the entrance of a building and waited until Lemming passed him; then he followed him at a distance. He continued to follow him until he reached the beginning of Bliss Avenue, where the old gate of the University Hospital was. Instead of going toward the Prep School in the direction of the lighthouse, Lemming walked to 'Abd al-'Aziz Street in the direction of al-Hamra. He stopped in front of the home of an American professor who was one of the old-timers at the university. Lemming used to know the professor's daughter very well, and she sometimes accompanied us to the Nuits Blanches and drank vodka with us. As he told Tom later, Lemming intended to enter her room and rape her. Fortunately, the effect of the hashish was beginning to go, and Tom was able to stop Lemming before he rang the door bell. Tom took Lemming to his room. Lemming did not resist because he had regained his old temperament and laughed and cracked jokes while Tom tried to put him to bed. As soon as he was in bed, he was overcome by a deep sleep.

-16-

In June of 1947, Lemming, Tom, and Singh decided to spend the summer holidays in Paris. The three of them left Beirut on board an old Greek ship and reached Venice after five days. From there they took the train to Paris. I did not hear from them until the end of the summer, when I received a postcard from Tom telling me that he and Singh would arrive in the middle of August (and that was the date I received the postcard), but he mentioned nothing about Lemming. In the afternoon of that day, Tom and Singh arrived by airplane but Lemming was not with them. Tom told me they were sitting one day at a café when Lemming said that he felt he was dispirited and anxious to return to New York. He immediately went to the hotel, packed his belongings, and took the first airplane to New York the very next morning.

I met Lemming in Washington three months later. He had been waiting for me at Andrews airport since the evening of the previous day. We spent about two weeks together in Washington, Richmond, Roanoke, and New York, parting in New York when I left for Chicago to go to the university and he stayed in New York looking for a job. Since then, I have seen him only three times.

The first time was in Chicago in the spring of 1948 after he had decided to enter the Unitarian Seminary, affiliated with the University of Chicago, to prepare for ordination in the Unitarian Church. During his studies in Chicago, he met a woman some twenty years older than he was and married her. Tom later told me that a stranger once approached Lemming at a social gathering, and said to him, "Your mother [meaning Lemming's wife] is really a young and beautiful personality."

The second time I saw Lemming was in New York in the fall of 1951 after I had moved to New York, completed my course requirements, and begun to write my doctoral thesis. At that time, I lived with Usama Qadri in his apartment on 27th Street in Manhattan. Lemming came by in the afternoon before Usama had returned from his work. We talked for a while, then I offered him a glass of whiskey. "Is it possible for you," he asked in surprise, "to offer me a drink that belongs to Usama, while he is absent?"

His behavior was odd. Hardly would he settle down in a seat when he would move to another, and he lit one cigarette after another. I did not know at the time that he was passing through the most difficult period in his life. He never mentioned that he was being observed by the Federal Bureau of Investigation and was unemployed because he was suspected of being a communist.

The third time I saw him was in Washington in 1966, fifteen years later. He had written to say that he expected to come to Washington to attend a certain conference and was looking forward to visiting me with his wife. He did not mention that he had divorced his first wife and had married a second. When he arrived in Washington, he telephoned to ask for directions to my house. Half an hour later, he was knocking at my door. Lemming was accompanied by a black woman whom he introduced to us as Mrs. Lemming. He had become fat. When we sat down to talk, I offered him a glass of whiskey, but he declined, preferring to drink a cup of tea. He smoked cigarettes nonstop. I learned that he was then living with his wife in Chicago, in the black neighborhood on the South Side of town, and that he had been unemployed for a long time.

Four years after that meeting, he called unexpectedly. I was preparing to leave Washington to join the American University of Beirut as a visiting professor for the academic year 1970–1971. My wife picked up the telephone, and I heard her in the next room saying in surprise, "Lemming. Hugo Lemming, you're in Washington?"

But he was calling from Chicago. He had read in a Black Muslim newspaper published in Chicago about a lecture I had given in New York, and about another I was scheduled to give at a conference to be held in Chicago in the following week. Lemming said in a trembling voice, "I am very eager to see you. I read your lecture and liked it very much. I'll attend the conference especially to hear your next lecture."

He spoke for a long time on the phone. I tried to shorten the conversation to lessen the burden of the long-distance charges. But he wanted to talk. His voice was becoming merry and joyful, and I was reminded of the Lemming I had known twenty years before. We agreed to meet in Chicago the following week. I hung up wondering what had caused the strong emotion Lemming had divulged; then the answer came to me in a flash. He had discovered, on reading my lecture, that I had a leftist tendency like himself and that he could now consider me—and for the first time after these many years—a friend he could trust. The conference to be held in Chicago never took place; it was canceled on account of the demonstrations that followed the tragic shootings at Kent State University. I left Washington for Beirut the following month, and that was the last time I spoke with Lemming. I don't know where destiny has led him.

-17-

As for Tom Shea, my relationship with him was, from the beginning, much stronger than my connection with Lemming. We were the same age exactly: we were born on the same day of the same month in the same year.

I remember well the time I first saw Tom. That was only a few days after he had moved to the Lodge. Before he put on his shirt, I watched him put some pleasant-smelling ointment under his armpit, and I thought it was some medicine. I did not discover that it was only an antiperspirant until several years later when my girlfriend bought me a box of it in New York and placed it in the bathroom without comment. Since that time, I have become accustomed to using it daily and, occasionally, I recall Tom Shea as I do so.

After I left Beirut in 1947, Tom stayed there and I did not see him until 1958 when he visited me in Washington. At the time, I was living with my first wife in a small apartment in Georgetown, just opposite the house of John F. Kennedy, who was then a US senator. Tom had gone through many experiences, and many things in his life had changed. He had traveled from Beirut to India after graduating in 1948. There he had moved from place to place until he settled down in Kerala. In the mid-1950s, he had returned to the United States and enrolled at the University of Pennsylvania in Philadelphia, where he earned a Ph.D. in economics. In Philadelphia he met a divorced woman in her early thirties who had a little daughter. He had married the woman only a few months before our meeting in Washington.

Tom arrived in Washington in the afternoon. I was waiting for him in my office at the university, and I took him home with me. I fixed us two dry martinis, which was then my favorite cocktail. We sat talking together for a long while—about the past and about the future. He told me that he had signed a contract with Aramco to work with the company in Dhahran, and that he was leaving for Saudi Arabia with his wife in a few weeks. He appeared to be really happy for the first time since I had known him. We drank several more martinis, and when suppertime came, Tom said he felt dizzy. He went quickly to the bathroom and threw up. A few moments later, he came out and apologized profusely. That was, he said, the first time he had ever been overcome by drinking (the way I had been in our undergraduate days). As for me, I was ready to drink another martini… How time transforms us!

Our second meeting was in Beirut five years later, in 1963. Tom had been granted a one-year leave of absence by his company to study Arabic at the Shamlan School. He moved his family from Dhahran and rented an apartment in Ras Beirut at the corner of Sadat and Hamra Streets. He spent weekdays at Shamlan and came to Beirut on weekends. I had also come to Beirut on a year's leave. I was writing a book in English on the revolutionary movement in the Arab world, and at that time I was single again. As soon as I met Tom, I could see that he was not happy—as he had obviously been when we had last seen each other in Washington. His old listlessness had returned. He introduced me to his wife and daughter, but I did not feel comfortable with them. His wife was tall, slender, and beautiful. Her daughter—blond, plump, and vivacious—was an adolescent who looked older than she really was.

Tom told me that he and his wife had agreed that each would lead a private life and would not interfere with the affairs of the other. In fact, during her stay in Beirut that year, his wife behaved like an unattached woman. In her husband's absence, she stayed up late at night and spent her time in the company of men. Rumors spread about her, including reports that she could be obtained at a price.

A short time before I returned to Washington, Tom and I sat down together at Dbeebo Café overlooking the Rocher, a place we used to frequent when we were undergraduates. We ordered two bottles of beer, and he said, "Do you remember the times we sat in this place, sixteen years ago? Everything has changed but not this place."

"The sea has not changed."

"The sea has changed, too. Look at the shore of al-Ramla

al-Bayda. Do you remember how white it was?"

Yes, I remembered. I looked at the sandy shore extending from the farthest point of the gulf to Saint Simon beach. It had all been transformed into a residential area. High buildings rose above it and a highway built along the sea carried speeding cars. The shoreline was filthy, garbage strewn all over it. The white sand could no longer be seen. Only a small, polluted strip of beachhead was left under the wall retaining the highway.

Tom said, "We have also changed."

"And does it sadden you that we have changed? We're both thirty-six years of age. This is the age of maturity, the age of achievement."

He looked at the cars as they sped on the highway running parallel to the café. I thought he had not heard what I had said, but after a while he turned to me and spat out: "Maturity...... achievement! I haven't reached the age of maturity... I'll never achieve anything in my life... I've grown older... and years keep passing. My life today is just as it was in the past; nothing has changed in it. Do you know that I can't sleep and that I'm ridden by anxiety and fear most of the time? I'll remain like this until the day I die. I'm sure of that."

I said, "Don't we all have sleepless nights? Aren't we all anxious? Why do you consider yourself alone in this?"

"Do you really know what sleeplessness is? Sleeplessness is to never sleep, night after night. I don't remember sleeping a whole night since childhood. Anxiety and fear! Anxiety and fear possess me day and night. I feel that an iron hand compresses my heart all the time."

"And what's the cause of your anxiety, Tom? We all suffer from anxiety and fear."

"I'm neurotic, I know that. And knowing it reduces the vehemence of my continuous pain somewhat. But the source of my pain is beyond my will."

Then he said something I did not expect: "The biggest problem I suffer from is sex. I think constantly of sex. There'll come a day when I'll lose my mind and plunge into the chaos which I feel I can't run away from."

Tom's fear turned out to be quite in order, for the day did come when chaos overwhelmed him and he did not know what he was doing. It was in 1966. He had come from Dhahran to Beirut for relaxation and was staying at the Phoenicia Hotel. I was told the details of what happened by a ranking officer of Aramco who was summoned to the Phoenicia at 1AM in order to take Tom to the hospital. Tom had been found naked in the hallway sometime after midnight, knocking at the door of a married Lebanese woman, whose acquaintance as well as that of her husband he had made the day before. When the woman opened the door, Tom tried to force his way in, but she shoved him out and shouted for help. Tom kept telling her in English, "I don't mean to hurt you. I only want to sleep with you." Apparently, he imagined that if he came naked to her, he would thus prove to her his sincere and innocent intentions. A few persons heard her loud cry for help, including her husband, who was coming up on the elevator. They jumped on Tom and gave him a sound beating, but Tom offered no resistance and surrendered completely.

By the time the police arrived, the bones of Tom's left shoulder had been broken and blood was flowing from his mouth and nose. The company officer took him to the American University Hospital, where he stayed several days under treatment. When he was discharged, Aramco sent him on to the psychiatric sanitarium at the Mayo Clinic, a famous hospital in the United States. Tom remained there several months until he regained his psychological balance and was able to return to his job in Dhahran.

After I had remarried, my wife Gayle and I visited him in Dhahran in April of l971. He received us at the airport. I sat next to him in the car, and we engaged in pleasant conversation. On reaching a high place overlooking the oil fields where the burning gas sent flames into the air, creating a terrifying scene, Tom said, "Look at the fires of Hell. They surround us on all sides."

His tone was serious and his voice, cool. I turned to him as I began to smile, thinking he was joking. But I checked myself when I saw him frowning, the muscles of his face contracted convulsively and his eyes burning with an odd brightness.

On the next day, I visited him in his office. He told me about his job and about his research, which he was preparing for publication. In the evening, we had dinner together at his little house, and we drank whiskey that he himself had made in his garage— like all Aramco personnel—because alcoholic drinks are forbidden in Saudi Arabia. His wife monopolized the conversation, and I was unable to speak with him. Two days later, we returned to Beirut, and I didn't see him again.

Two weeks after that, I received the news that Tom had committed suicide.

His wife had left Dhahran for the United States. At home alone, Tom had taken sleeping pills, put a record on, and lain down on the sofa in the sitting room. The doctor said the record was still turning when his Indian servant found him dead the next morning. On the table beside him lay a short note. It said that he had decided to commit suicide in full awareness and with determination. He also asked that his dead body be cremated and his remains scattered over the desert. He willed a sum of money to his Indian servant, and the remainder of his property to his wife. The company executed his will exactly, took his corpse to Bahrain and had it burned there at the only crematorium in the Gulf. His ashes were then scattered over the Eastern desert.

-18-

In the early part of my undergraduate life, I was under the influence of Mikha'il Nu'ayma and his mystical philosophy. I had begun to read his works in the last year of Preparatory School, after having read all of Jubran Khalil Jubran's books in Arabic and English. In that period also, I began to keep a journal of my observations on the books I read and the thoughts I entertained. I have recently found this journal among my papers.

I read it over yesterday. The eighteen-year-old who filled its pages held my attention. The journal contains no social or political concerns, and it concentrates on "spiritual" and personal matters. For example:

> Stronger than the power of the intellect and more influential is that of spiritual power through which many have been able to ascend to the realm of infinity. I do not understand the essence of this spiritual power because I have not experienced it. But my belief in its existence is strong because I believe in the philosophy of Mikha'il Nu'ayma, one of the greatest philosophers my homeland has produced. By possessing this spiritual power, he has reached heights that the intellect of the

senses is unable to reach. His happiness is perfect and complete: How can it be otherwise after Nu'ayma has seen the Absolute?

February 24, 1945. This is my feeling: There is something inside me which is about to choke me, and I cannot tear it out of myself.

March 16, 1945. I don't know what I can write in order to express myself. I have a feeling of a breakdown and collapse within me. Chaos in my mind and contradiction in my feelings shackle my will. I have now lost control of myself.

June ?, 1945. Summer has now begun. I must achieve an important goal this summer, namely, to define my view of existence and clarify the foundations of this view…

I joined the Syrian Nationalist Party the following year.

June 19, 1946. Today I joined the Syrian Nationalist Party. I joined it officially today, but I had joined it doctrinally when I studied the Party and understood it. This is a decisive step. It is decisive because of the responsibility which I took in joining this institution.

As such, it makes me now—as never before—an active member like many other active members who work toward a goal and are united by an ideal.

First of all, I have confidence in the doctrine that I adopted officially today. Second, I have confidence in the comrades and superiors I joined today. Finally, I have confidence in my Leader, whom I don't know in person but in the spirit and through the moral force embodied in the movement he created.

I have taken an oath today to be loyal to the Party and to my comrades in it, to obey the commands of my superiors, and to dedicate myself fully to the service of my doctrine and my Leader. I have taken this oath in the presence of my two friends and the Party, and here I am now taking the oath in the presence of myself. This is my greatest oath.

-19-

I do not intend in the following to diminish Mikha'il Nu'ayma's standing nor to belittle the value of his thought, for I still love and respect him. I became acquainted with him personally in 1943. I was sixteen when I visited him for the first time at Baskinta in the company of one of my friends from Prep School, 'Abd al-Karim al-Shawwa. I visited him a second time in the company of Fu'ad Najjar at the end of the summer of 1945, and I continued to be one of his faithful followers until I joined the Party.

Years passed and I met Mikha'il Nu'ayma again in 1953, by coincidence, over breakfast at the Alumni Club in Beirut. I was suffering that day from a ferocious headache caused by the many whiskeys I had downed at a party the previous night. I had no strong desire to talk. He asked me about myself, about America, and about my work at Georgetown University. I answered his questions almost curtly.

Then he said, "And how is your spiritual life? Have you found what you yearned for?"

I felt angry for no reason I knew. I retorted sharply, "These matters no longer interest me."

He looked at me with astonishment but said nothing. We finished our breakfast and each went on his way. But I deeply regretted my behavior. (Why do we behave rudely with those we love?)

In 1957 the first volume of his autobiography *Sab'un* (Seventy) was published while I was in Lebanon with my first wife, but I did not go to visit him, and I did not read his book. In fact, I did not read it until 1976, when I was writing these pages.

My last meeting with Mikha'il Nu'ayma was in the summer of 1960. I was having lunch at the Sinnin Fountain Café with a group of friends that included Adonis, Yusuf al-Khal, and Tawfiq Sayigh. Yusuf suggested that we visit Nu'ayma, who, as was his custom, was spending his summer at al-Shakhrub, which was only a few minutes by car from the fountain. Everyone thought it was a good idea, so we walked to him after lunch and found him sitting under the old oak tree, which he describes in the third volume of *Sab'un*. We sat with him for about one hour. His view of things had not changed. He repeated what he had said forty years earlier, with the same strict seriousness, his tone untinted by the slightest bit of humor. I remember being bound to his mystical ideas, ideas that filled my heart with warmth and my mind with emptiness. I now open his book *Al-Marahil* (Life stages) and I read the magic words that had captivated me in those years:

> In every face I see my own, because I too am subject to desires and passions, I am a victim of fears and a slave of time and place...
> Woe to my eyes, for wherever they turn they see only my own face. Greater woe to my face, for my eyes veiled with soil see nothing but the colors of the soil. I wish I could replace them with the eye that penetrates the curtains of time and place, the eye that gave me a glimpse yesterday of three human faces before which the specters of all human faces fade...

-20-

In the summer of 1945, I implemented in 'Akka a resolution I had made at the beginning of that year, namely, to write a philosophical study on what I believed in. I gave it the following title: "My View of Existence: Summer of 1945." I still have a copy of it and it is in English. I am rereading it today (November 9, 1975) for the first time in thirty years!

The introduction reads as follows:

> I must admit that what I am writing here is for the sake of my friends and not for mine alone. I am sure that my friends who will read these pages will do so with love and understanding, for these pages represent a great effort to accomplish a task which has not yet matured fully.

A thirst for my friends' praise and admiration!

I go on speaking about myself with the humility of one who is confident in himself. I discuss the subject in two main parts: in the first part, I treat the idea of God, and I declare in four pages that "knowledge" of God is not possible on the level of the intellect and science, this in support of the mystical ideas of Nu'ayma. Then I treat the idea of "man" and, in five pages, reach the conclusion that man's aim in life is the realization of happiness, as Aristotle said.

In the second part, I move to an analysis of my intellectual talents, and I admit with seeming pleasure that "I enjoy an organized, logical mind," in spite of the fact that I sometimes feel "a certain intellectual obscurity" that veils the light of the truth from me and makes my thoughts flow unclearly "like the waters of a muddy river." Then I enumerate the things that I find to be valuable in life and that deserve to be the aim of my work: "A few things make our living tolerable and sometimes endow it with beauty and meaning. The most important are friendship, love, art, reading, and work."

On friendship I say the following: "I cannot define friendship. All I can say is that friendship is based on mutual understanding, which ties two human beings with bonds of deep love." I cite Aristotle's saying that friendship cannot be general, "for he who has many friends, has none."

Regarding love, I declare with full certainty that "love is the most beautiful thing that is possible for the young to enjoy in life," and that "life through love becomes the most beautiful thing in the world." Then I point out, with some regret, that relations between young men and women in our Arab society is not as good as can be desired, "for the young women in our [young men's] lives are few in number, and this creates a lack in our lives."

Concerning art, I say that it is the source of the most delightful and the deepest of life's pleasures, if one knows how to appreciate it correctly. Correct appreciation requires high education. "Only through such high education can one truly enjoy the works of art."

On the subject of reading, I declare that the reading of books is "an inexhaustible treasure" and that for me "it is a fountain of joy that never dries up."

As for work, I consider it the most important thing in one's life, for in it "all other factors flow like streams into a river running to the sea, where it will find its great comfort." I distinguish between "creative" work and what I call "animal" work. In idealistic bourgeois language I say, "True work is not mere animal (manual) effort, but rather creative work with the most sublime aims and the highest meanings," i.e., intellectual work!

I end the study with the following summary:

All I seek in life is to live long enough in order to achieve the aims which I set myself and which realize my spiritual quests. I have great faith in myself, and he who feels the infinite power of the intellect feels this great faith in himself. My life will be a structure which will rise gradually, justifying my existence and adding to it the meaning and content of my life. I do not fear death, unless it comes between me and my work and thus prevents me from realizing my aims. When this structure is complete, I will have accomplished my task in life. When death comes, it will be a suitable end.

Among my study papers, I found a typewritten one on which the following was written in pencil in English: "My observations on Hisham Sharabi's study." These were the comments Hugo Lemming wrote in the fall of 1945 after reading my paper in Beirut. I read Lemming's observations anxiously and remembered our sessions and conversations at the Milk Bar, and all the good old days.

Lemming's sharp mind appeared clearly in these observations, as well as his Marxist tendencies, which I had not noticed in those days. He commented on every passage and on every page.

Regarding what I called "the Spiritual Kingdom," he wonders: "Through unconscious associations, we can prove the power of reason, the instincts, feelings, and fanaticism. As for 'the Spiritual Kingdom,' where can we find it?"

On my analysis of man's place in the universe, he says: "Your analysis of man's relation to the universe is the best thing I have ever read on the subject."

And on my conclusions, he says: "What you say here, if you care to know, represents my personal position exactly, no more, no less."

His final remark is: "In order that man may be able to realize his ideals, he must first have food, clothing, shelter, and some leisure. This is the main problem, and it has no solution but at the level of social action."

At the end of the summer of 1945, a week or so before the beginning of the academic year, I returned to Beirut. I went up to

Bayt Miri, where Fu'ad Najjar and his family were spending the summer in their home, which looked down upon Beirut and the sea. Fu'ad had built a hut on the top of the house and furnished it with two beds, one for him and the other for me. As soon as I arrived, I gave him a copy of my philosophical study. He leafed through it for a few minutes, then said: "Mikha'il Nu'ayma will be very pleased with it when he sees it."

We had planned to visit Nu'ayma the next day. In the morning, we took a car to Baskinta and arrived an hour later. Mikha'il Nu'ayma received us with his usual warmth. In the evening, he sat aside and read my study but he made no remarks on it until the next morning, when we went to al-Shakhrub and sat under the old oak tree. Nu'ayma expressed his admiration for what I had written, and especially for a poetic passage which he thought was my own verse. It read:

> Long is the night for one who cannot sleep,
> Long is the night for one who is tired,
> And long is life for one who does not feel
> The Eternal Spirit.

He said, "I particularly liked this passage. Congratulations."

"Unfortunately," I said, "it is not I who wrote this passage. It is taken from some ancient Indian writings."

"It doesn't matter," he said. And after a moment of silence, he added that he expected me to have a brilliant future in philosophy and said: "If I were to give you a mark, it would be an A at least."

In those days, Mikha'il Nu'ayma was thinking of establishing a circle or school of his followers which he would head, as do Indian gurus. He suggested the idea to us in the evening as we sat in his home, watching the rays of the sun change colors on Mount Sinnin. At that time Nu'ayma was in the process of writing *Mirdad*, in which he deals with the life and teachings of Mirdad, the wise teacher who returns to his birthplace after long absence in order to preach a new philosophy of life, is surrounded by a number of followers, and gains worldwide fame. Clearly, Nu'ayma saw himself in the role of Mirdad, having returned to the East (from the US) to preach and lead people to salvation.

Fu'ad and I were in another world. In fact, we were about to depart from Nu'ayma's ideas and enter into the thick of politics and violence as members of the Syrian Nationalist Party, leaving adolescence and its mystic dreams behind us.

-21-

Before I moved to the Lodge, I joined a secret society whose aim was the liberation and unification of the Arab homeland. To this day, I don't know who was behind this organization. Later on, it was recognized as one of several nuclei of the Arab Nationalists' Movement. Our cell consisted of a number of students from the freshman and sophomore classes. We met once a week in one of the dorm rooms and discussed different topics under the leadership of the person responsible for the cell. The meetings were long and the discussions boring. I became fed up after a short while. I had joined the society so as to extricate myself from the state of anxiety, uncertainty, and weakness I suffered from, not to exacerbate it!

I quit the cell and no longer attended its weekly meetings. I was still intellectually conservative and subject to the influence of traditional nationalism, the sort of nationalistic thought to which the previous generation, who had fought Ottoman imperialism, subscribed. That sort of nationalism fell victim to the British and French imperialism after the First World War and cooperated with it. My thought was concerned with slogans of liberty and independence, and it stopped at that. Yet, after I gave up my membership in the cell, I continued to thirst for a way out of my political loneliness. Important as it was, friendship alone was not enough to fill my need for communal belonging. The "I" and the "you" of personal friendship did not form, for me, the "we" in the correct communal sense. I yearned to become part of a greater whole, an entity in which my individual identity would merge with my general communal identity, and I thought that if friendship did not have such wider bond and deeper purpose, its potentialities would remain truncated and incomplete. All this—my conversation, my loneliness, my idealistic yearnings—led me in the end to join the Syrian Nationalist Party.

-22-

The immediate reason for joining the Party was a paper I wrote and presented in a political science course, during my third year of undergraduate studies. Our professor was Charles Issawi. He had asked me to choose a topic dealing with contemporary governments or parties. So I chose the Syrian Nationalist Party as a topic, not because I especially liked it, but rather to satisfy my curiosity about it, a party my freshmen cellmates had considered the greatest enemy of the Arabs and of Arabism. I spent months studying the Party and its history: I read all that had been written about it, I studied its doctrines and the speeches and articles of its founder Antun Sa'adah, who since 1938 had been a refugee in Argentina. I interviewed a large number of its leaders. I spoke at length with Ni'mah Tabit, the chairman of the Party at that time; I met with George 'Abd al-Masih, the first member of the Party, and with those responsible for its administration. They received me warmly and offered me all the help I needed. At the beginning of March 1946, I was invited with Fu'ad Najjar to attend the celebration of Sa'adah's birthday, March 1 being the most important official celebration of the Party. It was held at Ni'mah Tabit's home at al-Ghubayri, where the Algerian ambassador's residence now stands, near the airport traffic circle. The area of al-Ghubayri was outside the city of Beirut, to the south of the old airport and where the stadium stands today.

We arrived at Ni'mah Tabit's home at about seven o'clock in the evening. It was an old palace surrounded by a large garden full of the flowers of early spring. We entered the hall and found it crowded with young men and women. The atmosphere was saturated with a spirit I had never known. The meeting started with military discipline, greetings, and raised arms—in a manner that appealed to Fu'ad and me. Then speeches were delivered, the last speaker being Ni'mah Tabit, who spoke in a quiet and serious tone of voice. At the end of the meeting, I left the hall having shed all feelings of enmity toward the Party and developed a deep feeling of respect and appreciation instead.

I met with Ni'mah Tabit a second and last time. That was in the fall of 1946, about one year before he was expelled from the Party upon the Leader's return to Lebanon. I accompanied him on a trip from Beirut to the South to attend a series of party meetings in Tyre, Marj'uyun, and Rashayya al-Fukhkhar. We were accompanied in the car by a young Shiite man named Riyad Taha, who had recently joined the Party and who, after leaving the Party, became a prominent Shiite journalist and politician. He spoke to Ni'mah Tabit all the way and thus prevented me from talking to him myself and knowing him more, as I would have liked.

In spite of my intellectual shift from Arab nationalism to its opposite, Syrian nationalism, the emotional and intellectual atmosphere to which I gravitated did not much differ. The values, the concepts, the ideas were the same, although their alignments differed in some respects. After the passage of so many years, when I try today to analyze my intellectual development in that period and to explain the reasons I moved from one point of view to an opposite one, I find that I am incapable of explaining. The ideas that in those days represented to me the heart of the truth no longer mean much to me. The idea of the nation: what does it mean to me today? The history or the civilization of the nation, whether Arab or Syrian: how important is it? The ideas associated with this or that viewpoint no longer have a distinct value, as far as I am concerned. Today, what concerns me is not a set of abstractions, but the life of the suffering, the exploited, and the enslaved. All ideas, values, and aims that do not bear directly on the life of the people, of the masses, no longer affect me or mean anything to me.

-23-

The airplane carrying Antun Sa'adah to the homeland from Latin America after his nine-year absence from home landed on March 2, 1947. Thousands of Social Nationalists came to receive him at the old airport of Beirut in Bir Hasan, where his tomb now stands in the Mar Ilyas cemetery. Sa'adah was forty-two years old on that day, having left Beirut in 1938 at the age of thirty-three. It never occurred to him or to any of us on that day that his tomb would be in that spot—in about two years' time.

On the same airplane (arriving from Egypt) was Fawzi al-Qawuqji, who was himself returning to Beirut from Germany, where he had spent the war years. Al-Qawuqji mistakenly thought that the crowds at the airport had come to receive him, and so he waved and smiled at them as he stepped off the airplane. He did not discover that the crowds had come to receive Sa'adah until the latter appeared at the airplane door and the Social Nationalists began to cheer him and boisterously hail Syria. From my position outside the little airport building where I stood with Fu'ad Najjar, Labib Zuwiyya, and others from the university directorate who had come to greet him, I saw al-Qawuqji step aside to make way for Sa'adah, then follow him to the outer entrance.

The Leader and his retinue walked in a procession of thousands to the home of Ni'mah Tabit at al-Ghubayri. And there, Sa'adah delivered his famous arrival speech, in which he declared that the Party would never abandon its Syrian nationalism, that Lebanese isolationism and the sectarian system of Lebanon deserved to be attacked, and that the Fertile Crescent should unite in its struggle to liberate Palestine. Fu'ad and I stood near him, and his words continue to echo in my ears:

"This is the happiest day yet of my life as I return after nine years' absence away from you, and join this growing group representing a nation that has refused to accept the grave of history as a place for it in life. After fifteen years of unmatched and organized struggle, we stand today as a living and victorious nation, having triumphed over the foreign wills that wanted to keep us torn into religious sects and communities, all of whom believe in One Heaven. Our Nationalist doctrine has served us as a new and single religion, unifying and raising this nation to the One Heaven and to eternity in it."

The crowds applauded and shouted: "Long live Syria. Long live Sa'adah." I looked around and saw tears running down the cheeks of old Nationalists who looked motionless at Sa'adah as though they could not believe what they were seeing and hearing, and I saw some of them embrace others: "Sa'adah is back, Sa'adah is back, the Party is back."

He continued his speech: "What do the Lebanese want their entity to be? Resplendent with light inside and surrounded by darkness outside? If there is light in Lebanon, then this light should duly spread out and shine on all natural Syria."

Cheers rang out again. The name of Syria was pronounced publicly for the first time in the Party's history; in Sa'adah's absence it had only been known as "the Nationalist Party." Everyone wanted to call out at the top of his voice: "Long live Syria, long live Syria."

Sa'adah then moved to the subject of Arabs and Arabism.

"Your triumph was also over another false rumor, namely, that the Social Nationalists are the enemies of Arabs and Arabism. Yet, if there is true and genuine Arabism anywhere in the world, it is the Arabism of the Social Nationalist Party.

"What is this Arab League that represents the Arab world today? Is it the idea of the delusive and utopian Arabists who want an Arab empire and an Arab national unity? Or is it the implementation of what your Party has called for, namely, the creation of a front consisting of the Arab nations that stands as a dam against foreign imperialist ambitions and as a power with considerable weight in important matters of political decisions, and that can be the effective means to realize the wills of all these nations?

"The Arab League today is the realization of what the Social Nationalist Party has called for. We are therefore the advocates of true Arabism, and others have been those of false Arabism. Furthermore, we are the front of the Arab world, we are its heart, we are its sword, and we are its shield."

Cheers rose again to high heaven.

And finally he spoke about Palestine.

"Our struggle continues. You should always remember that Palestine, this southern wing of Syria, is very dangerously threatened. The will of the Social Nationalists is to save Palestine from Jewish ambitions and their consequences.

"You will probably hear people say to you that saving Palestine constitutes ill will against Lebanon and the Lebanese, and that it is a matter with which Lebanon has nothing to do. The saving of Palestine is, indeed, just as much a genuinely Lebanese concern as it is a genuinely Syrian and a genuinely Palestinian concern. The Jewish danger to Palestine is a danger to all Syria; it is a danger to all these entities.

"I repeat: these entities should not be prisons of the nation but rather strongholds in which the nation is fortified, and in which it prepares itself to pounce upon those who covet its rights.

"My charge to you, O Social Nationalists, is to return to the battlefield of struggle."[1]

-24-

We returned to the university with joyful and confident hearts. We did not discover until the following day that an arrest warrant had been issued against Sa'adah, and that he had refused to receive it and had sought shelter in the Mountain.

I met the Leader for the first time in the Mountain when he summoned Fu'ad and me to his temporary quarters in Bshamun. I remember the exact date of the meeting because it was my twentieth birthday. When we arrived, he received us warmly as though he had known us for a long time.

He had tremendous charisma, the effect of which is difficult to explain. Of average height, he had a well-built body, a dark complexion, sharp features, and penetrating eyes. He was in full control of his speech and movements: he did not raise his voice or gesticulate. In his dealings with all those he met, he was amiable and gentle. In all the time I knew him, I never saw him treat anyone harshly or arrogantly; he was, rather, always polite and extremely sensitive to other people's feelings. I don't remember that he ever ordered me to do anything. If he needed anything, he requested it indirectly by insinuation or by expressing the need for having something done, thus leaving the initiative to whoever was concerned. He dealt with all subjects and problems in this way.

When I returned from Chicago in 1949, two years after his return to the homeland and a few months before his death, Sa'adah learned that I was in love with an American girl and that I was thinking of going back to Chicago to continue my studies for the Ph.D. I will never forget the way he reacted. He did not say to me, "Forget the girl, for you have other duties you should perform." Nor did he offer me advice or impose his will on me in any way. Instead, he called me to his office and asked whether I had the time to spend the next day with him. I said, "Of course." On the next day, I went to his home near the Khalidi Hospital and found that he had prepared everything so as to spend the whole day on the beach and that he had borrowed Madame Rawdah's chalet on the Saint Simon beach. We swam and ran, and then we had lunch on the veranda overlooking the sea. We talked about various subjects, and finally he said:

"You know that emotion is something in our lives we should fight and overcome. If we don't, we can realize nothing important in life."

A little while later he said:

"I know how you feel, and I appreciate that. I myself passed through a similar experience. But I tell you in all honesty that, whenever there was conflict in my life between emotion and duty, I always put duty first and cast emotions on the ground and stepped on them."

That was all he said on the subject, and he never returned to it. I decided to stay in Beirut, and I postponed indefinitely going back to Chicago. But that was later, of course.

Our first meeting with Sa'adah in Bshamun lasted about three hours, and we talked about the need for intellectual work in the Party. He still felt stung by the fact that Fakhri Ma'luf had left the Party, adopted Catholicism, and joined an extremist religious group in Boston. Fakhri was the Party member closest to Sa'adah and the one he most loved. I don't think that he ever loved a person in the Party as he loved Fakhri Ma'luf. So when the latter left the Party, he also left an unhealed wound in Sa'adah's heart, which made him mention Fakhri over and over during all the period that I knew him. When I was in Chicago, I wrote to Sa'adah asking whether he had any objection if I contacted Fakhri. He responded in a letter dated August 23, 1948, saying: "Neither the Central Bureau nor I have any objection to your visit to the former secretary, Fakhri Ma'luf. But based on the information I have, I am inclined to believe that the only benefit to be derived from such a visit would be to learn his condition."

The letters Sa'adah sent from Brazil to Fakhri Ma'luf during the war are, in my opinion, some of the most important of his writings, explaining the idea of Social Nationalism and the philosophy of the Party. They were all later published in *Al-Nizam al-Jadid*.

When I returned to the United States after the Leader's death, I tried to contact Fakhri Ma'luf several times, to no avail. He had cut himself off from the world completely and had moved with his family and some of Father Fini's followers and their families to a farm about one hour from Boston, leaving the world behind them in order to be with their chief. Years later, in 1965, I met with him when I visited him in the company of his sister, Mrs. Fayizah, and I found that he had relented. He looked as I had imagined him to be: calm, gentle, sensitive, and intelligent. When I said goodbye to him, I felt I was bidding farewell to the last vestige in me of the Party, to something that had been part and parcel of my youth.

After I obtained my B.A. in philosophy in June 1947, the Leader did not object to my continuing my studies in the United States. On the contrary, he encouraged me. So I sent an application to Harvard University, another to the University of California at Berkeley, and a third to the University of Chicago; I was accepted by all three universities. I chose the University of Chicago because of its distinction in philosophy. But I did not leave Beirut immediately, and I postponed my departure until the end of 1947 so as to remain near the Leader as long as possible.

Toward the end of June 1947 and soon after my graduation, I went up to the Party's mountain camp at Dhur al-Shuwayr. The Leader was still "underground" because of the arrest warrant against him. From time to time, Public Security forces made surprise search raids on the places in the mountain where the Leader was said to be hiding. Every time they tried to capture him they failed, because news concerning the Public Security orders reached the Party almost as soon as they were issued. When we received word by telephone that Public Security forces were leaving Beirut for the place where we were, the Leader remained utterly calm and unperturbed. If we happened to be in the middle of an important meeting when the warning arrived from Beirut, the Leader would not leave the meeting place until the chief guard came to inform him for the tenth time that everything was ready and the car was waiting.

It was all completely new to me. At the beginning, I would be overcome by anxiety when we received word of a surprise search raid, and I would beg the Leader to end his conversation or work and to go to the car at once. Yet, even in the worst of times, Sa'adah was always calm and in full control of his nerves and movements. Nothing at all ever agitated him. While the guards were overcome by anxiety or confusion, he collected his papers slowly and put them in his briefcase, with which he never parted. He walked to the car with firm steps, said goodbye to those in the house, smiled, and waved to everyone as he stepped into the car, as if he were leaving a tea party.

One day we received a telephone call informing us that a large police force had left Beirut and was on its way to us at Dhur al-Shuwayr: it was about four o'clock in the afternoon. The guard went to inform the Leader, who had withdrawn to his room to rest after a long meeting over lunch that had drawn out past three o'clock. Minutes elapsed but the Leader did not leave his room. The guards were waiting at the entrance in three cars pulled up on the road alongside the monastery, ready to go. I became so anxious that I left my seat next to the driver, went back into the house, knocked on the door to his room, and entered. I found him lying on his bed reading a book. When he noticed how disturbed I was, he smiled and said, "What are you afraid of? Have you not become accustomed to surprise search raids yet?"

I said, "We've been told the surprise raid is a big one this time, Mr. Leader."

"Don't be afraid. Sit down," he said. "Let's have a cup of coffee first, and then we'll go. This time, we'll go to a place you will like. Do you know Baskinta? The place we'll go to is above Baskinta."

To drink a cup of coffee took us ten minutes, which felt like several hours to me. As he slowly drank his coffee, Sa'adah talked about the book he was reading. It was an English book about the history of the Sumerians. He said, "Do you know what prevents me most from reading? It's the thoughts that come to my mind as soon as I begin reading. I find myself trying to jump ahead of the author's thoughts, and thus I leave the atmosphere of the book completely."

In the fullness of time, we climbed into the car and headed for Baskinta by way of the Boulogne Forest, then down to Btaghrin and Wadi al-Jamajim. It was about sunset when we reached Wadi al-Jamajim. By the time we entered Baskinta, night had descended on the town. Its streets were empty and one could hear nothing but the murmur of water in the streams and the ceaseless croaking of frogs. We got out of the car, followed by the guards who were in the other two cars. Waiting for us were three or four men, who, I learned, were responsible for the directorate of Baskinta. We walked, climbing the mountain, for almost three hours, until we reached a dark hillside on which a tent was pitched. The Leader put his things in it, then went out to talk to the guards while I lay down to rest. I soon fell asleep and did not wake up until the next morning when I heard the guards bringing breakfast. The sun was still behind Mount Sinnin. I realized that we were on top of a hill that commanded a view of Mount Sinnin on one side and the sea on the other. It was a splendid place. It was everything the Leader had said it would be. The Leader awoke and sat on the wool blanket with which he had covered himself during the night. Breakfast was brought to us, and it consisted of yogurt spread, thin flat bread, and tea. I ate heartily and felt deeply overwhelmed with joy. The Leader looked at me and smiled, recognizing, without being told, the joy and happiness that filled my heart.

-25-

During that period, the Leader conducted the affairs of the Party in a businesslike, almost routine, manner in spite of our constant movements. He held regular meetings of the Council of Chiefs, and Council members came to his temporary quarters whenever he called them, carrying their briefcases and the files related to their various sectors. The meetings often lasted from sundown to the dawn of the next day.

At these meetings, the Leader eagerly examined everything. He dealt carefully and comprehensively with all matters raised, so that no question remained unanswered and no further issues were left undecided. He used to ask the Council secretary to read the official reports arriving from the directorates and from the executive districts, as well as letters received from Party members.

In the beginning, the chiefs used to come to the meetings with nothing in tow but their cigarette boxes, as though they were going to an evening party. But they soon understood the importance of these meetings and altered their ways. After the third or fourth meeting at the Dhur al-Shuwayr camp, the chiefs started bringing their reports and their papers to the meetings, and their assistants, too, to ensure that they would be prepared to deal with questions relating to their particular sectors.

The presence of the Leader brought about deep changes in the Party within a short time. A new life ran through it, and all over the country the directorates and executive districts began to be reanimated and to grow. Party delegations began to arrive from Lebanon, Syria, Jordan, and Palestine to meet the Leader.

In July, the weekly Party bulletin appeared, and its effect was like a bombshell. The Leader had given instructions to the chief of publications to print the Party's Storm emblem on the bulletin cover with the Party colors (black, white, and red). The emblem had not been used prominently in the Party during the Leader's absence. The appearance of the Storm emblem in this way was tantamount, therefore, to a new act of defiance against the authorities, a declaration that the Party had returned to the arena of struggle. It had a strong psychological effect on Party members. Old Party slogans revived, and the use of the word Syria spread; so did the Party greeting, "Long live Syria." Thousands of new members joined the Party, and dozens of new executive districts and directorates were established in Lebanon, Syria, Palestine, and Transjordan. After almost becoming Lebanonized, the Party, everyone felt, had returned to its true doctrine.

-26-

Sa'adah's personality had overpowered me so completely that it was impossible for me to conceive of questions such as those that Fayiz Sayigh, Ghassan Twayni, Karim 'Azqul, and others had begun to raise concerning matters of principle, doctrine, and organization. I supported Sa'adah 100 percent, refusing all criticism and opposition. I did not raise with him (as perhaps I should have) the subject of the change he had introduced into the doctrine after his return from Argentina. He came up with a new definition of the concept of the Syrian homeland: it now was "the Syrian Fertile Crescent," whereas earlier the concept of a Syrian homeland had been limited to historical Syria (i.e., Lebanon, Syria, Palestine, and Transjordan). He had added, in the new definition, Iraq, Kuwait, and Cyprus, and done it without referring the matter to the members of the Party or obtaining the approval of the Higher Council.

Likewise, swept along by his words, I unhesitatingly accepted intellectual positions that I would have hesitated to accept if left to myself, such as his ascribing a universality to society and considering society an ultimate ideal in itself; and his view that the individual was a mere means that society used to achieve its aims; and that society represented a firm and abiding "truth," whereas individuals fell away like autumn leaves; also his belief in a national economy based on capitalist production, without change in the ownership of the forces of production. I did not raise objections to the ways of thinking he practiced, but rather submitted to his views uncritically, as pupils submit to their teachers or a child to the authority of his father. Perhaps the reason was that I did not feel any aversion, as I do today, to pyramidical systems based on hierarchical authority. I was unable psychologically to oppose Sa'adah or to confront him negatively on any issue.

I believed in Sa'adah with all my mind and with all my heart. To me, he was the Leader, the hero, the ideal father. I loved and respected him as I loved and respected no one else. He will ever remain so to me, emotionally, even if I reach a venerable old age.

Had Sa'adah lived longer, he would be as old as Camille Sham'un or Pierre Gemayel today, i.e., in his early seventies. I wonder, had he lived, how long I would have remained a member of the Syrian Social Nationalist Party or remained loyal to it.

There is no doubt in my mind that, intellectually, we would have eventually parted ways. My relation to Sa'adah and the Party had to change from a dependent to a dialectical one. It would have been inevitable, the result of a process, of individual growth to maturity, psychological development, and the achievement of a certain level of awareness. At that point, values based on authority will inevitably encounter contradictory ones as they meet with a critical mind and as thought becomes free and rejects mere faith as a basis of the truth around which the individual's life revolves. And this is, in fact, what happened to me.

-27-

I would like here to point to a special aspect of Sa'adah's thought and concerns, namely, that aspect relating to the Palestine problem. To him it was the first national cause and he gave it more of his thought and effort than he did any other subject, especially in the last two years of his life.

Sa'adah's interest in the Palestine problem went back to his early youth, when he was in Brazil. He had written his first article on the Palestine problem in 1925, when he was 21 years old. At that time, seven years before the establishment of the Party, he considered Palestine an inalienable part of the Syrian homeland; and he did not differentiate between Lebanon, Syria, Palestine, and Transjordan—nor between these and Iraq and Kuwait after 1947. The Palestinian soil to him was part of the soil of his homeland, and the Palestinian people were part of his Syrian nation. After his return in 1947, he reorganized the Party branches in Palestine and admitted to their ranks an increasing number of Palestinian youths. It is certain that, if the 1948 war had not happened, the Party would have become within a few years a power to contend with on the Palestinian scene, and it might have changed the chain of events and perhaps prevented the catastrophe.

I have no doubt that Sa'adah's analysis of the Palestine problem, especially his political analysis, is among the deepest ever written on the subject. I would like to survey here some of Sa'adah's positions regarding the Palestine problem, and to present a few brief extracts that show the spirit of his writings. They form an essential part of my own intellectual history.

-28-

His first analysis was published in the Damascus newspaper *Alif Ba'* in 1931 on his return from Brazil. He was 27 at the time. It took the form of an open letter addressed to Lloyd George, the British prime minister, in response to a speech in which Lloyd George had said that the Jew living in Tel Aviv had as much right to protection as the Muslim living in Kanpur,[2] and that "Arabs and Christians" in Palestine had benefited greatly as a result of the success of the Zionist movement. Sa'adah answered in the following words:

> You know, as well as I do, that that country, Palestine, is a vital part of a whole, an integral part of an indivisible homeland belonging to one single nation, which is the Syrian nation.... As for your statement referring to 'Arabs and Christians,' it contains an error on which our newspapers sellers might reproach you; for there are no 'Arabs' and 'Christians,' but rather a community which is part of the Syrian nation that has a message, all of whose contents provide for the awakening of the Arab world as a whole.

> Grave consequences, very grave consequences will follow from this criminal attempt, whose like history has never recorded. I assure you that the results will not be limited to Palestine, but will involve the whole world, and that its immense aftermath will affect not only the Israelites but all humanity. And he who lives long enough will see.[3]

In 1937 when the Lord Peel Committee came up with its plan for the partition of Palestine into two states, one Jewish and the other Arab, Sa'adah sent a memorandum in the name of the Syrian Nationalist Party[4] to the League of Nations. The Party had been discovered by the authorities in 1935, having remained secret for about four years prior to that. In the memorandum, Sa'adah opposed the partition plan because "it ignored the Syrian people in Palestine," and he rejected the idea of establishing a Jewish state and declared that the partition of Palestine would lead to the rise of a Jewish state "the citizens of which would be able to admit Jews in numbers whose absorption possibilities were determined by them alone." He said that for Syrians to accept the drawing of the boundaries of the Jewish national home "required recognizing this home and the abdication of Syrian sovereignty rights over their own homeland, a material loss which the Syrian nation could not accept because this was a matter of life and death." He said that accepting the partition plan would open the door of immigration wide, permit the establishment of the racist Jewish state, and finally lead to the expulsion of the Palestinian Syrians even from the land that was specifically theirs. Partition "allowed Jews to increase their immigration and to make the territory of the Jewish state one hundred percent Jewish, thus completing the creation of a Jewish state on Syrian land, and expelling and scattering Syrians from the land designed for their own state...."

As for the financial compensations, which the partition plan suggested that Britain and the Jewish state should pay to the Palestinians in return for population exchange, Sa'adah considered them to be "ownership of this land by forced possession... a violation of the right of the Syrian nation and its sovereignty over its homeland, a breach of the unity of the Syrian homeland, and a usurpation of the best lands of the Syrians of the south..."[5]

The partition plan of the General Assembly of the United Nations of November 29, 1947 had a painful effect on Sa'adah. It confirmed what he had said about the inability of the ruling class in the Arab states and Palestine—"with its specific qualities, and its religious and tribal partisanships"—to face the Zionist danger and prevent the catastrophe. At the beginning of December 1947 (and I was still in Beirut), he issued a communiqué[6] in the name of the Party, in which he declared that a state of war existed, and he opened the opportunity for volunteers to join "the Social Nationalist Army":

> I declare that the Social Nationalists are today in a state of war for the sake of Palestine.
>
> All supervisors of training and all trainers should organize the Nationalists in platoons.
>
> All General Executive Bureaux and the directorates under their jurisdiction should have registers for volunteers who wish to join the Social Nationalists Army and fight under the flag of the Storm.
>
> Social Nationalists form an army by themselves; and, so, every Social Nationalist should join his platoon and his company.

When the Leader wrote this communiqué, I was with him at the office of the Party newspaper in Khan Anton Bey. When he finished writing it, we sent it to be printed and published in the newspaper that evening. We left the office together, and he was silent and frowning. When we reached home, a large number of Party members were waiting for him. They surrounded him, as I stood by, thinking of the situation we were in.

The catastrophe occurred and we had no sufficient power to do anything. He knew that perfectly well. Talk about the Social Nationalist Army, the declaration of war, and the opening of enlistment registers, all were only temporary palliatives to conceal our weakness and impotence. Here he was standing alone in the midst of the noisy crowd. His dream was to create of it "forests of lances over which fluttered the flags of the Storm," heroes like him who would not budge from the sublime aim but would face death with a calm heart and firm spirit. Fifteen years had passed since the foundation of the Party, and yet it was still an unrealized dream. I wonder, did Sa'adah purposely ignore bitter reality and permit himself to live in a dream?

One day at the beginning of 1949, I went to his home on a Sunday at his request, but I did not find him. One of the guards told me that he had gone to al-Ramla al-Bayda' to watch the maneuvers of the Social Nationalist troops. "Maneuvers... Social Nationalist troops," I wondered. I took a taxi to al-Ramla al-Bayda', which in those days extended from the point where Beirut International Hotel now stands to the Beirut forest and beyond. From a distance, I saw Sa'adah standing on a sand hill looking through military binoculars at a group of Party members doing military exercises under the leadership of a man I had never seen before. Sa'adah was wearing a semi-military outfit and was accompanied by the training captain or perhaps his deputy, I don't remember exactly.

Did he believe he had an army?

I remained in the sitting room until everyone had left. He invited me to have lunch with him, and when we sat at the table, he said: "Everybody wants war. What are we going to fight with? The Deliverance Army leadership is feudalistic, King 'Abdallah does not want to cooperate with us, and we have no arms or money..."

He was afraid to lose the Party by sending its small military force to Palestine. He wanted "those who announced they had prepared for war and said they were equal to it" to start their fighting. He expected they would be soundly defeated, for their threats in his view were "mere charlatanism" and their leaderships were backward feudal acts capable of nothing.

A few months later, when the traditional leaderships revealed their inability, he declared: "Our forces stand ready for the day when, by the people's will, I will make my announcement. We shall not be led to it passively by the policies of private interests and Western machinations."

But that day did not come. The Deliverance Army withdrew and the Arab armies were defeated. Then treaties were signed in 1948 and 1949 for a truce between Israel and the "confrontation" states.

In a letter he sent me to Chicago in the summer of 1948, he said:

It gives me great pain to be unable to save the national cause, which was and still is capable of being saved. The reactionaries understand nothing but their own language, and they want to know nothing but their own methods. Meanwhile, the majority of the people are under the power of a reactionary psychology. We have nothing left for us but to suffer, to continue our work, and to prepare the Syrian Social Nationalist movement for the duty of changing destiny...."[7]

His anger with the Arab regimes and their methods reached the point that he accused them of having fought in Palestine, not to save it but to occupy what they could of its land:

The war in Palestine was not a war with the Jews. The Syrian, Arab, and Egyptian armies which marched on Palestine did so, never to fight the Jews but rather to fight the Palestinians in their own land.... The war in Palestine was a conflict among diminutive states over what remained of Palestine, not a war to regain what the Jews had taken of Palestine.[8]

In that period, I believe he had become fully convinced that the only salvation was to take over the rein of government in one of the Syrian states and to establish the Social Nationalist State in it.

We cannot preserve the nation's interest and move on to external conflict to preserve the nation's external interests before we are able to end the internal war. It is a violent war, a war between the nation's will and several private wills.

In a speech he delivered a few weeks before his death, he attacked the ruling classes and called for the establishment of the Social Nationalist State. He described those ruling classes as "the internal Jews" and announced that the Zionists had not defeated the Syrian Nation but rather its "internal Jews" did, and he said:

As I announced the future establishment of the Jewish state because I foresaw that Syrian weakness would inevitably bring it about, I announce today the future destruction of this very same state. The announced destruction of this state will come about, not through a leap of illusive imagination, but through the ideological and party structures that the Social Nationalist Party is preparing to make of Syria a great military power that knows that the victory of interests in the struggle of life is determined by force after being determined by right.[9]

His vision now became clear: It would be "the Syrian Social Nationalist State" that would liberate Palestine, not "the dwarfish governments" who were not worthy of "shouldering the responsibility of determining national destiny." And for the first time, Sa'adah announced that the Party was training its members militarily and that it would be capable of fighting Israel and consequently all the regimes that "created" Israel.

> The Jewish state today graduates military officers. The Syrian Social Nationalist state, which I declared in 1935, graduates military officers, too! When the armies of the new foreign state begin to move in order to realize its aggressive designs and to seize the rest of the land of our fathers and forefathers, our armies too will move to cleanse the land of our fathers and forefathers and the heritage of our sons and grandsons from the defilement of that foreign state.
>
> This is not the last word we give, for the last word shall be on the battlefield after the National Leadership decides to declare war.[10]

-29-

From the time my father registered me at the age of seven as a boarding student at the Friends' Boys School in Ramallah and until I graduated from the American University of Beirut and left for the United States in 1947, I spent my summer holidays or the major part of them every year at my grandfather's home in 'Akka.

As far as I was concerned, 'Akka was (and still is) the most beautiful city in the world. In it I spent the greatest part of my childhood and the best days of my boyhood. 'Akka lies on the northern cape of the gulf of Haifa. Its name is an Arabization of the French name, Saint-Jean-d'Acre, used since the time it was occupied by the Crusaders in the eleventh century. The old city still retains visible traces of the Crusaders, especially the strong wall which surrounds it. 'Akka still looks like a Crusader city forgotten by time when one views it from the sea or from land (from Napoleon's Hill, the artificial elevation that Napoleon built in 1799 in order to shell 'Akka with his artillery). The wall surrounding the old city still stands, unchanged. The Ottomans encouraged the building of houses outside the wall in order to enlarge the city. They also established the Municipal Park at the turn of the century: it is a large park in the tradition of European public parks. In the middle is a kiosk for the band that, every Friday afternoon, played martial music and songs. The Ottomans also built the railway station opposite the Municipal Park along the shore, just outside the Eastern Gate. We rode on the little Ottoman train on many a trip to Haifa, which took 45 minutes. To the south of the station is the sandy beach where we used to swim on Fridays and Sundays. I have visited many parts of the world and saw many sandy beaches, but I have never seen a beach that equaled the beauty and splendor of 'Akka's. Its sand is snow white, its gulf water is clean and blue, its waves are quiet and wide, and they break gently and smoothly. The beach was always empty because the people of 'Akka did not like swimming and preferred to spend their leisure time sitting on their balconies and porches, or at cafés, or going out for walks at sunset. Thus, the beach was left for us to enjoy as we liked, to share with nobody other than a small number of visitors from Haifa and the soldiers who came from the British barracks near the city to swim daily for an hour in the afternoon.

The city had two cinemas: one in the old city, called al-Burj Cinema, and the other in the new city, called al-Ahli Cinema. The former was merely a large hall built on the city wall overlooking the gulf near the Eastern Gate. We used to see American cowboy or detective movies there. On leaving the world of American imagination, we found ourselves suddenly in the medieval era, surrounded by Crusader and Islamic ramparts and battlements. We heard the echo of our footsteps in the empty ancient lanes and alleys as we returned home, arriving at midnight when everybody was asleep.

My room opened directly to the sea. My bed was near the window, and so I slept and woke up to the roar of the waves. From the sound of the waves breaking on the rocky shore, I could tell whether the sea was stormy or quiet, and whether it was good for fishing or for swimming.

We used to fish on the weekend. My two fishing companions, Kamil and Akram, didn't return from their jobs until the afternoon, when fishing was not very good. But during weekends, we woke up early and hastened to the shore. We fished until sunrise; then we ate our breakfast and went to the sandy beach near the Railway Station in order to swim and surf to the end of the day. When the weather was good for fishing on weekdays, Kamil absented himself from work, calling in sick, and we spent many hours fishing and going from place to place until noon. Those were incontestably the happiest days of my life. Sometimes we caught a lot of sea perch or striped mullet, and sometimes we caught nothing. When we had a good catch, we enjoyed a magnificent dinner of fried fish in the evening with parsley-and-sesame-cream salad, fried bread, chickpea dip-salad, and eggplant dip-salad prepared by Kamil's mother. We ate dinner on their roof. After dinner, we went to the movies or sat at Habibuh's café and drank sodas, played backgammon, cracked jokes, and watched the girls as they walked by, holding each other's arms, laughing, and stealing coy looks at us.

My grandmother, God bless her memory, used to love me very much. She never gave birth to boys and so, next to my grandfather, God bless his memory, I was the only man in her life. She used to worry about my secluding myself daily in order to read and write for hours on end. In her view, it was something unnatural. She was especially worried when I sat on the porch alone, motionless and wrapped in thought as I looked at the sea. She would come to me on the porch and ask me tenderly, "Why are you sitting alone, my love? Do you have a headache? Do you have a fever?"

Her only remedy for all sicknesses, psychological as well as physical, was chamomile. She used to impose it on all members of the family, especially on me and my grandfather. Chamomile is a wild herb that, when boiled in water, turns into a tea-colored drink that is very bitter. My daily portion of it was the three or four cups that I drank unwillingly at my grandmother's insistence. She always waited for my arrival, and when she saw me coming down from the roof or returning home from anywhere, she poured me a cup of chamomile tea and faced me with it: "Drink this cup, my dear. May you have health."

"But I'm not sick, grandma. My stomach doesn't ache, nor is there anything wrong with my head!"

"Drink a cup for your grandma's sake… or half a cup only."

And when I told her that too much chamomile tea made me constipated, she said, "What nonsense! Who ever said that chamomile causes constipation? On the contrary, it keeps your bowel movement going, and it protects from all diseases."

And when I complained of too runny a bowel movement, she would bring me chamomile tea and declare, "There's nothing like chamomile tea to stop diarrhea."

In addition to the comprehensive medical protection that she gave me through chamomile tea, my grandmother used to give me strong spiritual protection through continual prayers and invocations. She believed firmly that I was indebted to her for my life because of her prayers and invocations and that, had it not been for her, I would never have escaped the dangers of the outside world—which she only knew from her window or from the few visits she paid to the families who, in her view, were of equal social status. It used to give her pain to see me shrink from performing my religious obligations. So she used to compensate for that by doubling her own acts of worship for my sake. When I was ten or eleven, she tried to reform my religious affairs by applying a direct method (it was her first and last attempt). She sent me to the shaykh of the small mosque next to our house in order to learn the principles of religion. For a reason I still don't know, the shaykh scheduled our lesson at dawn every day. I woke up daily at four o'clock or thereabouts, when it was still dark. I put my clothes on quickly and ran to the mosque, where the shaykh would be waiting for me, cleaning his teeth with a toothpick. He made me read from a book whose title I don't remember. It dealt with acts of worship and religious obligations such as ablution, prayer, and fasting. After I read the lesson to him, he began explaining what I had read.

My religious studies did not last long. The reason they were cut off was my refusal to practice *tayammum*, which is ablution with earth instead of water. One dawn we had reached the topic of *tayammum*. I did not know what it was and had never heard of it. The shaykh started explaining the circumstances in which it should be resorted to instead of ablution with water.

"This drawing illustrates the circumstances in which we ought not to expose our souls to perdition, and in which *tayammum* is in order."

He said this, pointing to an illustration in the book which showed a lion with unkempt hair, standing angrily in front of a pool of water in the desert.

"This drawing shows the correct way of *tayammum*."

And he indicated another illustration showing a man covering his face with dust in a manner that looked in the picture like a little sand storm; the man was standing at a distance from a lion and a pool of water. We spent the remainder of the class discussing *tayammum* and the circumstances in which it was advisable and permissible. Thus if you were traveling in the desert, and prayer time arrived but you found a disheveled lion standing between you and the ablution water, then you would know what to do... My grandmother did not insist that I return to the shaykh after I told her about the lion and the dust and the circumstances in which *tayammum* was or was not permissible. She was afraid that, if the shaykh continued to teach me, I would lose what faith I still had.

My grandmother was thin. She had a white complexion, reddish hair, and light brown eyes. Doubtless, she had been extremely beautiful in her youth. She had a strong personality, and my grandfather did not oppose her in anything and submitted to her commands, though he was sometimes obstinate with regard to smoking and coffee. My grandmother permitted him to smoke half a cigarette and to drink half a cup of coffee at specified times and in accordance with a meticulous daily program. He always tried to gain more concessions, such as smoking a whole cigarette or drinking a whole cup of coffee. Their life was quiet and happy, especially after they moved to their new house.

My grandmother always dreamed of owning her own home. This dream of hers was realized in the l930s after she had saved enough money to build a large house. She commissioned a young architect to build it, named Emile Bustani, who after the Second World War became the biggest construction contractor in the Arab world. He built her a most modern house, though the bathroom did not function as perfectly as one would have wished.

My grandfather and grandmother left their home in 1948, and

that was the hardest experience of their lives. The last years of their lives were full of sorrow, despair, and a feeling of loss. My grandmother lost her joy and vitality, and my grandfather lost his reason and no longer recognized those around him. My grandparents stayed with my aunts, my mother, and my youngest brother in Beirut in a house that had two rooms, a house owned by a woman who was distantly related to my grandmother.

My grandfather died in 1950. Before his death, he tried from time to time to sneak out of the house to return to 'Akka. When they caught him in the street, he used to say, "I'm only returning to my home... My home is in 'Akka... Why don't you let me go back home?"

He used to take a key out of his pocket and say, "You don't believe me, do you? This is the key to my house."

When they brought him back in, he sat silently, tears flowing from his eyes and wetting his beard, which my grandmother no longer cut as she had in 'Akka. And he would refuse to speak for a long time after that.

My grandmother died eight years after he did.

-30-

Faces from the past appear in my imagination at this moment: Antun Sa'adah's face as he delivered a speech to a dense crowd; Mikha'il Nu'ayma's face as he read in the light of sunset; Charles Malik's face as he lectured in the classroom....

Many other faces appear before me, faces I loved that vanished from my sight a long time ago: the faces of Tom Shea, Hugo Lemming, Jakmahang Singh, Yahya Homsi, and Fu'ad Najjar.

And two faces I have never seen that do not leave me: Nietzsche's and Kierkegaard's.

-31-

A few days before leaving for the United States [in 1947], I stopped in 'Akka to bid farewell to my grandfather's family, my mother, and Kamil and Akram.

I had left Beirut by car on a very cold December day. Before sunset, we arrived at the British checkpoint at Ras al-Naqura. After being checked, the car continued on its way down to the village of al-Zib. The sun was about to set. In the twilight, I could see the city wall of 'Akka and the minaret of al-Jazzar Mosque rising above the city in the gray sky. Behind it was Haifa and Mount Carmel sloping down to the sea. I opened the car window a little and felt the cold wind brushing my face. I began looking at the rough waves of the sea, which reminded me of summer days, fishing, swimming, and merriment. I saw a sailboat dashing through the waves and leaving a long white line of froth in its wake as the wind filled its two sails. It was going from Sidon or Tripoli to 'Akka.

The road was empty except for one or two buses of the Eggèd Jewish company as they sped to reach Naharia, the only Jewish settlement in western Galilee, before dark. When lights were just beginning to be turned on, we were on the main street in 'Akka. In Habibuh's café, there were only a few people playing backgammon. At the entrance of al-Ahli Cinema, I saw nobody, perhaps because the movie had not yet started or because it was a cold day.

My grandfather had gone to bed, so when I arrived home, I sat with my grandmother, my maternal aunts, and my mother. They were all apprehensive because of my imminent departure. I ate a light supper consisting of yogurt spread, cheese, and olives, as had been my custom in 'Akka since childhood. After supper, it was about seven o'clock, so I put on my overcoat and went out to see Kamil and Akram at their home next to the café.

They were waiting for me behind the door to surprise me with their military preparations. One of them was wearing a military helmet like the ones British soldiers wore, and he carried an old hunting rifle.

After we sat down, Kamil said, "Have you heard about the incident?"

"What incident?" I asked.

He told me how the people of 'Akka had attacked a Jewish caravan on its way from Haifa to Naharia. A number of armed young men had ambushed it at the crossroads of the Beirut and Safad routes. The caravan consisted of five armored cars and several trucks. When it arrived, they showered it with bullets. Their goal was to damage the lead car, forcing the caravan to come to a halt, and then attack the remaining cars. But the bullets did not penetrate the steel plating of the armored car at the head of the caravan, so it continued advancing, although its tires had been punctured by bullets. The driver or his companion fired on the trenches on both sides of the road from time to time. One of the young men in the trenches shouted, "Sam'an al-Ghifri, where is he? Call Sam'an al-Ghifri."

Sam'an al-Ghifri owned the only modern automatic machine gun in 'Akka. They found him in an ambush on the other side of the crossroads. He rose immediately and crossed the road to where the armored car was passing, by the garden of the Habayib house. He jumped over the garden wall, walked parallel to it with his back bent until he reached the place where the armored car was going slowly. He propped his machine gun on the edge of the wall and fired. Moments later, the armored car was ablaze and its driver and his companion jumped out of it onto the road with their hands up in surrender. The armed young men began firing from all directions on the other cars, which had now stopped. A few minutes later, the Jews began jumping out of their vehicles with their hands up above their heads. All the cars of the caravan surrendered except the last armored car: its occupants continued to shoot. The armed young men surrounded it and concentrated their fire on it. A little while later, the armored car stopped shooting and its driver waved a white handkerchief. So the young men rose from their trenches cheering joyfully. Hardly had they taken a few steps when the armored car hailed them with bullets. Several were killed or wounded, and the others hurried to their trenches. They resumed their attack on the armored car until they set it on fire and killed its occupants.

I asked Kamil and Akram about the prisoners and they said they did not know what happened to them.

-32-

I left 'Akka on my way to Jerusalem early in the morning of the next day. Kamil and Akram had already gone to their work in Haifa.

I will never forget what Kamil had told me the previous night, as he said goodbye:

"When you come back from America, Palestine will have been liberated. All the Arab states are with us. The Deliverance Army alone is capable of occupying Palestine."

About two months after I arrived in Chicago, I received a letter from Kamil with photographs of him and Akram on the roof of their house with helmets on their heads and rifles in their hands. They stood there looking at the camera with confidence and pride, but the accompanying letter did not reflect the confidence that appeared in the photographs. Most of the inhabitants had left the city (just until the troubles would end, as Kamil said). Meanwhile, the Jews increased the intensity of their attack on Haifa and the neighboring villages and fortified Naharia and the border settlements. The letter bore no trace of Kamil's former merriment nor of his usual sense of humor.

In April of 1948, the impossible happened: the Jews occupied and chased out the inhabitants remaining behind, except those who took refuge in the old city.

My grandfather's family left at the beginning of the Jewish attack. Kamil and Akram remained in 'Akka until the last minute, and did not leave it until after the Jewish forces had entered its suburbs. They carried what they could and left with their mother and two younger brothers to the nearest town across the Lebanese border.

What happened? In May the morale was still high because a detachment of the Deliverance Army led by Adib al-Shishakli had arrived to defend 'Akka. People were encouraged and refugees from Haifa began to have hopes of returning to their homes. But al-Shishakli soon withdrew with his detachment, following orders from his commanding officer. People became disheartened, and despair became prevalent again. Food supplies were becoming low, and the fighters' ammunition was almost depleted. Bread and bullets were being sold in the black market at exorbitant prices. Al-Shishakli's promises to send help and reinforcements were not realized. Al-Shishakli's forces and the Zionist Jewish forces fought in the neighborhood of Safad. Al-Shishakli sent word to 'Akka seeking help, and the armed men of the city hastened to send him help in the remaining cars. When they returned a few days later, the wounded were taken to al-Jazzar Mosque, where some of them died because of the lack of medicine. Those who could not escape when the city fell were taken prisoner. As for al-Shishakli, he withdrew with the remnants of his troops across the Lebanese border, leaving the whole of western Galilee to the mercy of the Zionist Jews.

Kamil and Akram and their family first took refuge in Rumaysh, a village across the Lebanese border, where they rented a small room in an old house for an excessive price. Then the village became filled with refugees, and its inhabitants soon refused to offer them any more food and water. Water became so scarce that a can of water was sold for two Palestinian pounds. Kamil and Akram decided to return to 'Akka to see how things were. They stole away across the Lebanese border and reached 'Akka before sunset. When they found nobody in the streets, they went directly to my grandfather's house, where a family related to Kamil and Akram had taken refuge. They entered the house in complete darkness, the electricity (and water) having been cut off from the city.

Their relative, 'Adil, informed them of the situation: "All the people have fled. Those remaining outside the wall were forced by the Jews to leave town or take refuge in the old city."

Kamil asked him about food.

"There is no food. Everyone is hungry."

Kamil asked, "How about you? Will you remain behind?"

"Where can we go, with all our children? We have relatives neither in Jordan, nor in Syria, nor in Lebanon. We will stay behind."

Kamil and Akram then wandered about with 'Adil in the nearby street, and saw nothing but cats mewing with hunger. Kamil lunged for a cat in jest; it arched its back and bared its teeth.

It was clear that making a go of it in 'Akka would be impossible. Kamil and Akram bade their relatives farewell and returned to Rumaysh.

-33-

A few days before the fall of 'Akka, a number of armed men, Sam'an al-Ghifri among them, occupied the Taggart Building, the British police stronghold outside the city wall. They continued to resist the Jews for several days and inflicted many losses on them. They stopped fighting only when they ran out of ammunition. Some of them were killed; others managed to slink into the old city and then escaped to Lebanon by sea. I read the news of the fall of 'Akka in the *New York Times* on the day after the event, as I sat on a park bench in Chicago, watching children play baseball.

Those who have visited 'Akka recently say it is a big city today, extending several miles outside the wall. As for my grandfather's house, it is still there, and it is inhabited by a Jewish family. My Jewish friend Uri Davis recently sent me a photograph of it. I did not recognize it at first because there were no more trees around it, and its windows had been blocked on the street side. It appeared to me as things appear in a dream: familiar, but strange at the same time, in another world. The nearby mosque where I learned my first Qur'anic lessons is still there, too, but since the shaykh left it, it has been desolate. The remaining Arab inhabitants have been forbidden to live in the new city, outside the wall, and have been forced to live within the walled old city, which has become a casbah to the Jews, visited by foreign tourists wanting to buy locally made articles and to see "the Arab population of Israel."

—*Three*—

-1-

It continued to snow after my arrival in Chicago. People said the winter that year was more severe than usual. As far as I was concerned, it was not only a matter of mere cold. I could hardly go out at all. As soon as I did, an icy wind buffeted me, my nose froze, and my ears pulsed with pain. I thought they would freeze solid and fall off.

Ah for my homeland! Ah for its blue sky, its good air, and its warm sun!

In the first weeks, I left International House only for absolute necessities, such as going to the classroom or the library. When the temperature was a little above zero, I went across the I.C. [the Illinois Central park] to the little café, the Dirty Spoon Café as we called it, to have a cup of coffee and a piece of apple pie.

In the first semester, the winter semester of 1948, I took four courses, three of which were in the philosophy department and one in the German studies department.

The first course I chose in philosophy was "Aristotle's Philosophy," taught by Richard McKeon, the most famous American philosopher in the field of Greek and Latin studies. The second course was entitled "Pragmatic Philosophy" (from Peirce to Dewey) taught by Charles Morris, one of the leaders of pragmatic philosophy in the United States and professor of philosophy at Chicago and Harvard at the same time. The third course was "Kierkegaard's Philosophy," taught by Jean Wahl, professor of philosophy at the Sorbonne, who was a visiting professor that year at the University of Chicago; he was one of the bastions of the existentialist school in France and author of *Études Kierkegaardiennes*, which continues to be the principal reference for the course I took in the German studies department; it was a book on Kierkegaard's philosophy and existentialist thought. As for the course I took in the German studies department, it was on Nietzsche's philosophy and was taught by Arnold Bergstraesser, an anti-Nazi German professor who had come to the United States before the Second World War and whose specialty was the social sciences; in time, a strong friendship arose between us.

-2-

McKeon held his class in a middle-sized room on the second floor
of Swift Hall, a building designated for the philosophy department.
His was the first class I attended at the University of Chicago. It
had twelve or thirteen M.A. and Ph.D. students, all Americans, of
both genders. As soon as I sat down, McKeon, a man of moderate
height, entered the classroom, went to the platform, and began
looking at us through his thick glasses with a faint smile fluttering
on his lips as though he may or may not be mocking us. He then
began to count his papers and arrange the books he had brought
with him. I could hardly believe that I was a student in his class,
that I would be learning philosophy from him. He had a charis-
matic personality, as I later confirmed. He had been appointed as
the United States representative at UNESCO, which was to hold its
first session in Beirut in 1948 (the UNESCO edifice in Beirut was
especially built for this meeting). I wrote to my friends in Beirut,
informing them of McKeon's visit, and they received him warmly
and Fu'ad invited him to the 'Ajami Restaurant and introduced
him to a number of writers and others interested in philosophical
matters.

After the lecture that day, I went to the philosophy library,
which was still separate from the central library and occupied a
whole floor in Swift Hall. I checked out McKeon's works, which
were not many, and I read them all—with difficulty at first, then
with increasing understanding. Four or five weeks later, it became
possible for me to follow his lectures and understand them more
easily. McKeon asked us to take the philosophical text as the only
source in our studies, and advised us not to use the secondary
sources, written by commentators and scholars, until we had full
command of the text itself. To me, this was a radical transformation of my study method, and I used this same method later with
my students, when I became a professor myself.

McKeon's methodology had a deep influence on my intellectual orientation. I became more capable of distinguishing between
what was subjective and what was objective, and more adept at
using methodological analytical tools with increasing care. This
orientation was strengthened by a tutorial entitled "Reading of
Texts" that I took in the following semester with a young professor

in the philosophy department named Berry. I met with him once a week and we read Aristotle's *Ethics* and Hobbes's *Leviathan*. The method employed in the "Reading of Texts" tutorial was deceptively simple: the student read the assigned text by himself, then read it again with his professor sentence by sentence. The professor commented on the reading and analyzed the concepts and categories occurring in the text, until the student arrived by dialectical method at a full understanding of the text and its "language." In this manner, we read ten pages from the book of *Ethics* and no more than fifteen from *Leviathan* during the whole semester.

Only a few months passed before I grasped the principles of critical liberal culture, which the American University of Beirut had failed to teach me. I also began to perfect those two difficult arts: the art of reading and the art of listening.

-3-

Jean Wahl was a short man and had a small body shaped like Sartre's. Like Sartre, he wore round eyeglasses, but he did not squint like him. When he sat on his chair in the classroom, his feet barely touched the ground because his legs were so short. And although he spoke English fluently, his thick accent made his words seem obscure and sometimes incomprehensible.

His teaching method was the classical European one, based on lecturing. He avoided discussions in the classroom. He used to sit at his table and deliver his lecture. It filled the whole class hour—without stopping or providing an opportunity for questions or an exchange of ideas.

From Wahl's lectures, it became clear to me that what I had studied in Beirut of Kierkegaard's thought and existentialist philosophy was very little and hardly worth mentioning, exactly as was the case with Aristotle's philosophy. It became evident to me also that the study of Kierkegaard required knowing Hegel's philosophy, my knowledge of which did not go beyond a few general themes. My professors in Beirut had not even mentioned Hegel to us, perhaps because they did not know him or care for his philosophy.

Wahl used to take a text and examine it word by word. He posed questions and answered them himself until he reached the conclusions he sought, formulated in clear and precise points.

Wahl's lectures soon put an end to the romantic tendency nourished in me by the way we had studied Kierkegaard in Beirut. I too became more concerned with primary sources and with their texts, instead of depending on the explanations and analyses of commentators.

I mentioned to Wahl one day that the Egyptian philosopher 'Abd al-Rahman Badawi had authored a book on existentialist philosophy entitled *Al-Zaman al-Wujudi* (Existential time). He expressed interest in it and suggested that I take Badawi's book as the subject of my research paper for that semester. A few weeks later, I presented my paper to him, in which I reviewed the principal points of the book and translated a few passages from it.

Wahl called me to his office after reading my paper and said, "The book is ordinary. The translated passages and Badawi's ideas seem to be derived mostly from Heidegger's book *Sein und Zeit*. There is nothing new in them."

In the spring semester, I chose another subject and entitled my paper "The Kierkegaardian Dialectic: Truth and Existence." I have found it, with Wahl's remarks, among my papers. It seems he liked it, for on the first page of it he wrote: "Your ideas are clear and your style is strong (except for a few paragraphs I pointed out on pages 1 and 2)." He filled the margins with remarks and commentary, using three standards to evaluate my analysis of Kierkegaard's philosophy: Clear, to denote the passages he liked for their precision; Right, to express his agreement with me in opinion; and Good, to point out texts he considered outstanding.

Wahl particularly liked the last part of my paper and wrote GOOD in capital letters in the margin. I don't remember now whether this passage was a result of my own independent thinking or derived from other books without reference to the source. In it I presented a summary of the existential dialectic in Kierkegaard's philosophy, describing individual existence as threatened by contradictions and disputed by situations of "uncertainty, risk, passion, anguish, longing." I ended the paper in the following manner:

> To the individual existing thus, finality, in whatever form it comes—historical, natural, scientific, speculative—breaks down at the fact of the fluttering moment of decision. Passionately striving, infinitely longing, and

inwardly isolated, the existing individual is grounded in a situation which the existential dialectic reflects and accentuates; it is one permeated with opposites, constantly surging with becoming, everlastingly changing according to the unique situation: Illusiveness,[11] uncertainty, risk, passion, anguish, longing formulate true grounds of this existential situation. The existential dialectic strives to capture and represent the situation thus.

During Wahl's residence in Chicago, a tragic event happened to him that shook us all, but he faced it with tremendous courage. His wife, a young woman who had been one of his students in Paris, gave birth to a baby boy a short while after their arrival in Chicago. One morning, Wahl woke up and found the baby lying motionless on its back. He touched it and discovered it was dead. The baby's covers had become wrapped around its neck during the night so that it could not breathe. It had died of strangulation. Wahl did not absent himself from his class on the following day; he lectured us as if nothing had happened.

-4-

I don't remember how and why I chose to take Charles Morris's course on pragmatic philosophy. There were more students in his course than in McKeon's or Wahl's. The atmosphere of Morris's class was merry, and a spirit of familiarity and geniality predominated in it. On entering his classroom for the first time, I felt I was entering a café, not a philosophy class: the students exchanged jokes, laughed, ate sandwiches, drank Coca Cola, and smoked. When Morris entered the room, the students did not change their postures or stop talking. Morris sat at his table on the platform, then turned to one of the students and said: "What kind of sandwich are you eating? I've never seen a sandwich of this size!"

His method differed completely from that of McKeon or Wahl. He avoided the lecture format and gave ample opportunity for dialogue and discussion. It was his custom to move from his chair on the platform to a seat among the students, and so the students talked to him and conducted discussions with him as if he were one of them. Sometimes discussions became quite heated, but without causing any strain or tension, and they always ended with humor and laughter, in which Morris participated with natural spontaneity.

At that time, Morris was in his mid-forties. His name had begun to be known in academic circles after the publication of his book on the philosopher George Mead. In those days, he subscribed to Sheldon's theory positing that the basis of personality was the physical constitution of the body. A short, fat individual belonged to the endomorph group; a tall, thin one to the ectomorph group; and a person of moderate height and strong muscles belonged to the mesomorph group. The first was good-tempered, merry, and carefree; the second was high-strung and easily ridden by anxiety; and the third was inclined to deep thought, seriousness, and hard work. Each of these groups had a specific pattern of behavior. The first group, the endomorph, was characterized by contentment and satisfaction, its members' aim in life being to secure an easy living. The second group, the ectomorph, did not accept life as it was and had difficulty dealing with others, its members being inclined to isolation and solitude. The members of the third group, the mesomorph, differed from both by being practical in their methods and aimed at achievement in their work and behavior.

My knowledge in the social sciences was limited at that time. I did not realize how superficial Sheldon's theory was, and its narrow parameters escaped me. For more than 25 years, the social sciences remained at a remove from me—until the early 1970s, when I spent a good deal of effort studying them. My book *Muqaddimat li-Dirasat al-Mujtama' al-'Arabi* (Prologues to the study of Arab society), published in 1975, was a partial outcome of that effort.

In my research paper for Morris's course, I chose to compare existentialist philosophy with William James's philosophy. When I presented it to Morris, he liked it very much. On returning it to me, he said, "Nobody has ever dealt with this topic, and your treatment of it is excellent. I suggest that you publish it in one of the philosophical journals."

His compliment pleased me and restored to me a lot of self-confidence, which I had almost lost during the first icy months in Chicago. From that day on, I began taking a greater part in class discussions; no longer did I sit there silently most of the time. A strong friendship arose between Morris and me, and we began meeting each other outside the classroom over a cup of coffee or for a walk on the Midway after the weather warmed up, and we talked about diverse matters. These conversations had a strong effect on me, for Morris gave me—through his clear empirical insights—what I was greatly in need of at that time, namely, a new intellectual direction that would extract me from the metaphysical and idealist intellectual world I had been born into. Even so, pragmatic philosophy did not save me from the idealist tendency of my thought, but a new intellectual horizon opened in front of me, and outlines of new ways and methods were revealed to me.

A few months after I had returned to Beirut from the United States, I received a letter from Morris (in the spring of 1949) informing me that he was traveling to Japan to attend a scholarly conference and that he could pass by Beirut on his way back, if that suited me. I wrote back immediately and invited him to Beirut; I met him at the airport a few weeks later. Before his arrival, I had reserved a room for him at the Normandy Hotel, which, in those days, was in the same class as the luxurious Saint George Hotel. However, he preferred to stay in a second- or third-class hotel, not because he wanted to economize but because he hated first-class hotels. So I took him to the New Royal Hotel, which was in the neighborhood of the Normandy and opened directly onto the sea. It was a hotel where merchants from Aleppo and Damascus stayed, and where artists working at the Lido and the Kit Kat night clubs resided. We left Morris's luggage in his room and headed for the university. In the evening, I took him to Faysal's Restaurant, where a number of friends joined us, including Joseph Salama, Fadluh Khuli, and Nabih 'Atiyya (who emigrated to South Africa at the end of that year). Nabih had a bottle of French cognac, which he opened, offered us each a glass, then put it under the table. Morris drank his glass in one gulp, so Nabih poured him another. Morris drank it in a similar manner as he continued talking, so Nabih poured him a third, then a fourth, and so on until Morris had consumed the whole bottle, meanwhile showing no effect of the drink. When we reached the New Royal Hotel on foot, Morris remarked as he said goodbye to us: "Please, thank your friend who brought the cognac. Tonight I will sleep soundly. Good night!"

He climbed up the hotel stairs with firm steps, and I remembered what he had once told me in Chicago: that in one of his visits to certain islands in the Atlantic Ocean, he had eaten a dish of fried spiders and liked it.

A few hours before his departure, I took Morris to meet Sa'adah. Morris sat in the reception hall, and I entered the Leader's room to inform him of our arrival. I found Sa'adah shaving as he dictated his weekly article for publication in *Kull Shay'* newspaper. When he finished, he received Morris with his customary kindness, and he spoke to him in English—with difficulty but with precision and clarity. Morris was happy with the meeting and admired Sa'adah instantly and immensely, a fact that pleased me enormously.

-5-

The professor closest to me during the whole period of my studies at the University of Chicago was Arnold Bergstraesser, professor of German history and chairman of the Committee on the History of Culture, which I joined during my doctoral studies. Bergstraesser had left his country in 1938 and taken refuge in England, then moved to the United States and taught at several universities before ending up at the University of Chicago. During the Second World War, he wrote a book in English on modern German history. The Jews attacked him severely because he did not speak evil of the German people and their culture. They demanded that he be dismissed from the university, but the president of the university at that time, Robert Hutchins, stood by him and Bergstraesser remained in his faculty position.

During his residence in the United States, from 1938 to 1951, Bergstraesser continued to feel he was in a foreign country. He did not seek naturalization as an American citizen, as did his Jewish German colleagues at the university, such as Hans Morgenthau and others. In his lectures, Morgenthau would refer to himself in his thick German accent, saying, "We Americans." But I never heard Bergstraesser even once say anything that gave one to understand he was not a German. On the contrary, whenever he said, "We," it was clear he meant, "We Germans."

He was a conservative liberal in his political outlook and a staunch enemy of Nazism. After the war ended, he looked forward to the moment when he could return to his homeland and start his life anew, although at that time (in 1949) he was 50 years old. He was married to a German woman and had a daughter who was ten years old and spoke both English and German fluently. His greatest fear was that, after the Nazi defeat and unconditional surrender, the Allies would deprive Germany of its heavy industry and impose an agricultural system on her, as Henry Morgenthau, the Jewish secretary of the treasury during President Roosevelt's administration, requested in a famous memorandum published at that time. And despite Bergstraesser's strong opposition to anti-Semitism, he was against Zionism and feared the consequences of the quickly rising Jewish influence in the United States at the end of the war. He did not express his anti-Zionist feelings publicly and used to avoid the subject, but he discussed it with me when we were alone.

Bergstraesser returned to his country in 1951 and was appointed as a professor at the University of Freiburg. We remained in touch with each other until he died in 1967. He invited me several times to visit him in Freiburg. Every time, I accepted his invitation and began to prepare for the trip, but something always happened at the last moment to prevent me from traveling. I visited Freiburg finally only after his death, and went to the institute named after him at the university, the Arnold Bergstraesser Institute for Political Studies, which is one of the most important university institutes in Europe today for the study of contemporary politics.

In the first semester, I chose his course, "Nietzsche's Philosophy." Immediately after the first class, I went to the bookstore and bought Nietzsche's works collected in one volume, in the Modern Library edition. I still have this book and have thumbed it this morning. I reread some of the passages we studied with Bergstraesser and perused the remarks I wrote in the margins during class discussions and lectures.

Bergstraesser woke up very early in the morning and held his class at 8AM. All during the first semester, I got up at 6:30AM three times a week, took a bath, had my breakfast, and read a little to clear my mind of the night's dreams. Then I put on my heavy overcoat and my earmuffs, went out into the bitter cold, and walked knee-deep in the snow. The classroom was in the Harbor Building, not too far from International House, but the trip took me about twenty minutes because of the snow. Classrooms were overheated to the point of suffocation, and we were not able to adjust the temperature. If we opened the window, the icy cold invaded us, and if we closed it, the heat became unbearable. Meanwhile, Bergstraesser paid no attention to the matter. We opened the window for a while, then closed it and took off the layers of sweaters we were wearing, only to put them on again, and overcoats too, when the cold returned to the room. However, in spite of the early hour and the bad weather conditions outdoors and in the classroom, I managed—for the first time—to understand Nietzsche's philosophy very well.

The bonds of friendship between Bergstraesser and me became stronger in the first weeks of the winter of 1948. He often invited me to a cup of coffee at the drugstore or to lunch at the faculty club, where I later worked as a waiter for a short while when my financial resources had run out. Sometimes, we went off-campus to an Italian or Chinese restaurant on 55th Street. I used to dread these outings and attempted to avoid them, because they required using Bergstraesser's old car. It was not the car that aroused my fears but Bergstraesser's driving style, especially on snow-covered streets. He turned the car on, as I sat next to him, stepped on the gas pedal, and let the car dart forth and skid violently on the ice. Unconcerned, he talked philosophy to me, turning one eye in my direction from time to time, while I sat frozen in my seat fearfully looking forward. I nodded now and then, signaling my agreement with what he had said, until we reached the restaurant. He stepped on the brake and the car staggered left and right, sliding on the ice for a few meters and stopping by colliding with the rear of the car in front of it. When we finally sat at the table to eat, my appetite was gone and I ate very little.

Nevertheless, Bergstraesser was like a psychological savior to me at the time. I don't think I would have been able to overcome the difficulties I faced in the first few months as quickly as I did had it not been for his kindness, encouragement, and help. He was an elder brother and a friend on whom I could depend. I have been dependent on others all my life and needed their help and sympathy, and I have not yet fully gotten rid of this tendency.

Whatever were the psychological causes that nourished my relation with Bergstraesser, there were also basic intellectual factors that united us. Bergstraesser had a deep influence on my intellectual transformation. Among my old papers, I have found a letter that I sent him on February 14, 1948—that is, six weeks after the beginning of my studies with him. In this letter, I commented on his method of teaching Nietzsche and I surveyed the points by which we should be bound, and I said: "Your method of presenting Nietzsche's thought and of rationalizing him leads, in my view, to killing the unique side of him. Nietzsche writes in parables, not analytically. He writes in the language of magic. That is why the treatment of his writings should be in the spirit of Zarathustra, i.e., in a positively committed spirit."

Then I surveyed the conditions that one must follow, the most important being that the professor should be, in the words I used, "Nietzschean" in his thought and method.

> I believe that it is impossible for a follower of Nietzsche—a professor lecturing on Nietzsche must be one of his followers—to discuss his thought in a classroom without allowing Nietzsche's spirit to dominate the discussion completely. This cannot be achieved unless one highlights the existential side of Nietzsche's life in the imagination of those studying him seriously and in depth: showing his suffering, his sickness, his difficult isolation, his permanent infatuation with the Alps, and his living in rented dark rooms in Italy…. It is possible to kindle the fire of philosophy in the hearts of students, when their professor himself understands Nietzsche's thought and when its light burns in his own heart. I believe that raising up this light that illuminates all Nietzsche's philosophy is the basic condition to understand Nietzsche as a philosopher, a poet, and a prophet….

I ended my letter with these words: "My dear professor: I end these remarks by wishing you, as a professor teaching Nietzsche's philosophy, many intelligent students who are capable of sitting under 'the tree on the hill.'"[12]

Two days later, I received Bergstraesser's response. Perhaps I will not be exaggerating if I say I have never received a letter that has had on me the intellectual impact this letter has left in my soul; for it made me face a problem of methodology that I had never faced before.

In his letter, Bergstraesser contradicted all that I had learned at the American University of Beirut. He said:

> In this age, the university cannot permit itself to depart from any position but that of unbiased criticism with regard to the way it poses intellectual issues and the methods it deals with them. Dealing with Nietzsche's philosophy in the committed manner you suggest in your letter utterly contradicts the aim and task of the university…. Following such a method will inevitably lead to adopting a biased attitude toward every philosophy or intellectual trend, for it presupposes that the professor should be a believer in that philosophy or intellectual trend, and should teach it as a doctrine and faith. This in turn will lead to the undermining of the independent cultural institution, the foremost principle of which is to preserve a common intellectual language and an ability for mutual understanding based on objective analysis and open dialogue.

In his letter, Bergstraesser distinguished between two things: the cultured person's need to have specific intellectual and ideological positions, and the university's task of providing him with the intellectual and analytical tools that enable him to take these positions on clear intellectual bases. He said:

> The task of the university centers on ensuring the scholarly opportunity for the educated person so that he may be able to understand the issues discussed in our present age and analyze them in a sound and critical spirit…. Placing limitations on this educational task of the university raises some doubt in the minds of the young people about the value of university education. The university does not offer them the solution they seek, but only the method and the way. What you say in your letter expresses a general feeling, yet the situation in which you are may be an open and creative one if those experiencing it have sufficient courage and determination to face it. It is a situation arising from an acute intellectual crisis that does not accept easy solutions, especially those offered by theories claiming to have the whole truth. The courageous and determined stance

required in this situation is not only in admitting its surrounding difficulties and risks, but in seeking to reveal them, to face them, and to go along with them one step 'forward' in order to overcome them and transcend them.

He ended his letter saying:

Any other way may give a person rest and satisfy his psychological needs, but it will lead him to accept a narrow 'sectarian' outlook, and this will lead to the creation of numerous intellectual sects. An intellectual sect creates in man a limited intellectual foundation with a limited legitimacy; at the same time it negates the existence of a general truth that the human mind can understand and comprehend.

I would like to discuss these matters with you in person. Please, give me a telephone call between 8:00 and 9:00AM on any weekday.

In time, the objective methodology which I began to grasp in the first months after entering the University of Chicago enabled me to recognize and rid myself of the stains of my past education, and by means of it I took big intellectual steps "forward." But I did not arrive at a critical attitude toward an objective methodology and did not discover its role in supporting the dominant way of thinking and the prevalent sociopolitical reality until many years later. The non-objective aspects of "scientific objectivity" escaped me at that time and concealed from me the intellectual truth of its so-called neutrality, which hides a presumed prior commitment to a certain viewpoint that reflects the dominant ideology and its abstract contemplative nature, traits that characterize all bourgeois thought.

In short, I did not see through the conservative liberal stances taken by most of my professors. I accepted them without question. My thinking became saturated with an American (the Anglo-Saxon) liberal outlook; I adopted a position hostile to communism and the Soviet Union; and I accepted the theory of free enterprise and parliamentary democracy without any hesitation or reservation.

However, it was in this period that the antiquated psychological molds ingrained in me by the old social acculturation I had brought with me were broken. And Bergstraesser was the direct cause of that, as he was of my move from the study of philosophy to the study of history and European culture. This move was perhaps the most important step I took in my university education: I got rid of the abstract philosophical outlook I had grown up with and consequently I was spared the fate of the professional philosopher. New horizons and paths opened before me and led me to discover the social sciences and their perceptible scientific principles, concealed from me by the idealist existentialist philosophy that exalts itself above all that is scientific and perceptible.

-6-

In the 1960s, after I had become a professor at Georgetown University, I formed a strong friendship with a colleague of mine named Heinrich Roman, similar to my friendship with Bergstraesser at Chicago. Like Bergstraesser, Roman was a non-Jewish German and, like him, had emigrated from Germany because of the Nazi regime. We used to sit at a café near the university that was frequented by students. It was called Tehan's and was owned by a Lebanese man named Tahhan. We drank beer there and talked. I used to ask Roman about his life in Germany, about the First World War, and about Nazism. We talked about many of the subjects that I had talked about with Bergstraesser. When Roman was about to retire, the university board conferred on him the title of distinguished university professor.

He was fond of smoking cigars, so whenever I got hold of Havana cigars (forbidden in the United States at the time), I gave them to Roman as a present. He smoked cigars continuously. One day, he felt pain in his chest, so he took himself to the hospital and underwent several tests. He was told he had lung cancer and was forbidden to smoke. His disease was so advanced that there was no hope of his recovery. But Roman continued to teach until the last day of his life.

One day, before he entered the hospital for the last time in the fall of 1966, we were walking together on the university campus. It was cold, and autumn leaves were falling down all around us. I asked him about his health. He answered briefly as though the matter no longer concerned him; and he said everything was all right. Then he turned to me and added:

"I have made all the arrangements for my wife. My life insurance, my pension. And I have registered the house in her name."

His wife was a German woman who was short and spoke English with a thick accent as if she had just arrived from Germany. Her manner, her speech, her gestures gave the impression that she was lost and didn't know where she was or what she was doing. Roman spoke about his wife with some passion and anxiety, like one who felt separation was imminent.

He spoke to me about the past, about his student days, about how he met his wife, and about their life together. This sick old man appeared to me to be a young man in the prime of his life, full of strength and vitality. He spoke about his wife as if she was still the beautiful young woman he had fallen in love with more than 40 years earlier. He saw himself as a youth at that moment. How time defeats us! We grow old, yet our hearts remain as they have always been. Time doesn't change them, and the love and pain we have experienced abide in them. The further we advance in years, the more the past comes closer to us with its sorrows, its joys, and its memories.

He said, "Before our wedding, I said to her: I can't promise you a life full of happiness and joy, but I promise you, solemnly, it will be a life full of enjoyable adventures. And I have fulfilled my promise to her."

I saw him for the last time at Georgetown Hospital, lying in bed in a state of semi-consciousness because of the anesthetic drugs he was given to kill the pain in his chest. He looked up at me and did not recognize me at first. He closed his eyes, then opened them slowly as the shadow of a smile appeared on his face.

"Do you want to know how many cigars per day I smoke these days?" he asked.

(I had always asked him: how many cigars have you smoked today?)

I smiled encouragingly, "How many cigars? Tell me."

He turned his face away, trying to control himself because of the pain. I didn't know what to do. I couldn't do anything. I felt that a dear friend was about to leave and I couldn't say goodbye to him. He was about to leave without a last word reminding him of the love that bound us together.

On the day Roman died, I saw his wife coming back from the hospital. She was walking quickly with her small steps. When I approached her, I saw that her eyes were red with weeping. When she saw me, she stopped, and I asked her, "What can I do for you?"

She looked at me and said nothing. I don't think she recognized me. She said, "Thank you," and went on her way.

In the first few months of studies at the University of Chicago, I suffered a lot from intellectual indigestion. The courses I took in the first semester were more than I could possibly understand. While Bergstraesser dealt with materials from the historical cultural point of view, Morris dealt with them from the pragmatic point of view, and McKeon and Wahl from the analytical philosophical point of view. In the classroom, I often felt as though I were in a dream, especially during the first few weeks, and I did not fully understand what was going on around me. My loneliness added to my confusion. However, I patiently endured my loneliness and bore my intellectual indigestion. I had no choice, until the clouds began to disperse and things slowly began to be clear.

I don't remember a professor ever entering the classroom in Chicago empty-handed or giving his lecture while fingering his keychain as our professors in Beirut used to do, except for one professor, namely, Morgenthau. Morgenthau used to give his lecture impromptu without making a mistake in content, expression, or mental organization. He lectured as if he were reading from a written text before him. He cited figures, dates, and quotations by heart. I regularly audited one of the courses he gave, though I had not officially chosen it. I also attended his public lectures, which he gave in the largest of the university halls. He entered the public hall, his hand in his pocket, and he stood in front of the audience as he did in the classroom; and he gave his lecture for a full hour without stopping and in a charming literary style. He used to write his articles in the same manner: he dictated them to his secretary as he paced to and fro in his office, and she typed them and gave them to him ready for publication.

Although he was Jewish, he did not say a single word at the

time to give the impression that he sympathized with Israel or supported Zionism. Perhaps the reason was his ambition to become an advisor to the State Department or the White House, as his German Jewish colleague, Henry Kissinger, later was to do. But after he retired and lost all hope of having a government post, he showed his true colors as a thorough Zionist.

-7-

I was constantly on the lookout for public lectures and for special seminars held weekly at the university. My favorite seminar, which I attended every week, was held by the Committee on Social Thought. It took place every Wednesday evening at 8PM in a room on the second floor of Harbor Hall. At the seminar, usually no more than twelve or thirteen people were present, mostly students. They all sat at a round table that filled the room; the proceedings were headed by John Neef, chairman of the Committee on Social Thought. Neef began the meeting by introducing the student whose task it was to deal with the subject of the day's session. After the presentation, which took about an hour, discussions began, and anyone present wishing to participate could do so. In these meetings, I used to sit silently and follow what was happening without daring to participate. Discussions were always quiet: there were no emotional outbursts, and differences of opinion never became verbal battles. Differing viewpoints did not lead to clashes and contradictions, but rather motivated discussants to offer additional detail and to clarify their positions, and consequently they led to a better and deeper understanding of the subject. My American colleagues were all my age or slightly older, and they dealt with the issues under discussion with confidence and equanimity, talking to Professor Neef without fear or circumspection, as though he were a colleague of theirs. I compared my bashful and diffident behavior with their natural and confident behavior, and I wondered about the reasons for this difference but was unable to find the answer.

A number of Arab students attended the social thought seminar from time to time. One of them would attend once or twice, then drop out. Their number in any one session never exceeded two or three, and they were mostly students of economics or political science.

They sat next to one another, whispered to each other, and laughed. When one of them took part in the discussion, I was so embarrassed that I wished the earth would open up and swallow me. For he always presented his opinion in a categorical and definitive way, in broken English, and in an emotional and rhetorical tone. Neef always gave them an opportunity to participate in the discussion, and he listened to them carefully, which added to their conceit and made them go to extremes in their comments on the ideas he presented and the positions he took.

In that seminar as well as outside it, I had the opportunity to observe the behavior of my Arab colleagues closely, and to compare it with that of my American colleagues. The first thing that drew my attention in the Americans' behavior was their spirit of commitment and their sense of responsibility. To the American student, study and reading and preparation were basic duties to which all other considerations were subordinated. When he was alone in his room or in the library, nothing stopped him from studying and reading, and he did not permit himself any rest or entertainment until he had finished what he had to do. The Arab student's behavior was completely contrary. He was always ready to put his books aside if he had an opportunity to have a cup of coffee with a girl. His sense of responsibility was related to something outside himself, to an authority above him, not to an internal motive that bound him autonomously. When this outside authority (his father or his professor) was absent, a chaotic tendency replaced it and made him shirk responsibility and seek pleasure. Whenever he found himself free, he was unable to use his freedom.

To this day, I still feel that there are two stern eyes observing everything I do and evaluating everything I turn out. I still experience the fear and anxiety I used to feel as a schoolboy. And I always wonder: Am I wrong? Have I said anything to anger anyone? Have I done what is proper and necessary? I always expect to be judged and evaluated by others. My view of myself is constituted by how others view me. As I write these lines, my memory takes me back to preparatory school and to our teacher walking up and down the aisles between the desks, dictating to us whatever occurred to him. We wrote what he dictated, letter for letter and word for word. If a student committed an error, he stopped walking, held the boy by his ear, and twisted it to hurt him. After all these years, I sometimes hear myself unintentionally asking questions of my university students like those my teachers used to ask of us and in the same arrogant manner, as though like my teachers I want to remind them who really has the upper hand.

-8-

Many Arab students failed in their university studies and were unable to obtain the advanced degrees they desired because the educational system they had grown up in limited their ability to grasp basic principles in their fields of specialization and circumscribed their comprehension of Western intellectual methods. A few of them succeeded in obtaining higher degrees, not through their own efforts, but because of the American professors' compassion for foreign students and their readiness to evaluate these students' academic efforts by lower standards than they applied generally. Those Arab graduates returned home carrying doctorate diplomas but without much change having happened in their minds. Still, the title "doctor" endowed them with scholarly status, which permitted them to propagate their derived and unperfected thoughts among members of the younger generation. Had their American professors realized how their benevolent treatment of them would lead to such bad results, they might not have been so indulgent.

But there was another group of Arab students, a minority, who succeeded in adapting themselves and performed their academic duties perfectly, without requiring special treatment. They earned their degrees with hard work. They represent the good leaven, those who had been liberated by their new culture and who, on returning home, had done their best for their society without haughtiness or arrogance.

What mostly drew my attention on comparing the Arab students' behavior with that of their American counterparts was a specific phenomenon I could not analyze at that time, namely, hypocrisy. Arab students dissimulated and tried to deceive even their own Arab colleagues. They did so spontaneously, unconsciously. When an Arab student was asked by an American about himself, his family, his hometown, or any other matter, he lied or otherwise tried to deceive in answering. It became evident to me that this phenomenon was caused by the lack of a clear sense of identity. He who cannot take a definite position toward himself, his past, and others often tries to pretend to be someone else. He lacks self-confidence and needs outside props: he fabricates and dissimulates without premeditation; he lies and deceives without feeling any sense of guilt.

-9-

Like my colleagues, I was confused and did not know what to do. But I began to overcome my condition by studying my Arab colleagues' demeanor and analyzing what I felt. I saw my own behavior embodied in theirs. This helped me to understand myself and, in time, to lessen my own inclination toward hypocrisy, which I have still not completely done away with.

I wonder how an individual in Arab society can really know himself when he is surrounded, from childhood, by individuals who don't know themselves and live in a world built on lying and deceiving themselves and others. Everyone I have come to know in my society wishes to be someone else, in one way or another. Each pretends to be a person other than the one he really is. He has no self-confidence and disdains himself consciously and unconsciously.

I was unable, at that time of my life, to penetrate the masks behind which my compatriots hid. I could not distinguish between a liar and one who told the truth, between a deceiver and one who was sincere. For a long time, I did not know anyone for what he really was. I knew others only as they appeared to me through masks and my naiveté.

My interior dialogue about the personalities of my Arab colleagues—about their childhood, their family milieus, their early experiences—reverted to me. I asked myself about my own childhood, and I considered events that had influenced my own psychological growth and the formation, such as it was, of my personality.

Reconstructing the past is a difficult proposition. But there is no escape from it. And if we want self-liberation, a return to the past is necessary—in order to expose it, then transcend it.

-10-

I earned my degree by the sweat of my brow, not by the compassion or indulgence of my professors. In a few months, I felt I had changed. But the transformation was limited to intellectual aspects primarily, for my personality did not change (it still has the same basic constitution it has had since my boyhood, when I began to read on my own and discovered that girls were another sex). My experiences in Chicago hastened my intellectual maturity: I became capable of critical thinking and more realistic in facing difficulties. This newly acquired realism enabled me to accept matters as they were and to put aside illusions (it also enabled me, in middle age, to accept the passage of years without regret or complaint: I am not made miserable now to know I have spent most of my life having realized few of my dreams and aspirations).

Where is the future we dreamed of and gave our lives to? It is today, our present. It is yesterday, of which only faint flashes are left, haunting us when we least expect them and reminding us of beloved voices that have vanished, beautiful faces that we have forgotten, and an old love that we have lost.

In our children's eyes, we see the specters of our dreams as young ones, and in their smiles we perceive the images of the future that we left behind us.

In those months in Chicago, I discovered that I was an introvert by nature and a neurotic who gave himself up to anxiety and depression. I also came to know the limits of my potential, and this made me eventually choose a pattern of life that agrees with my nature and my potential, namely, university teaching, writing and scholarly research, and an introverted lifestyle.

-11-

In his autobiography, *Ecce Homo*, Nietzsche says that he avoids books and reading when he is engrossed in writing. He says, "To read in the early morning when one is, like dawn, at the summit of one's powers is an evil act." He adds, "He who cannot think unless he has a book in his hand loses his power to think independently, and his thinking becomes a mere reaction to the outside factors and influences."

I am one of those people who cannot think unless there is a book in his hands. All my ideas, in one way or another, are products of what I read. Not a single idea emanating from me can be described as an original or inspired idea. Everything I write is a result of continuous work and many hours of research, reading, and thinking. Writing an article or preparing a lecture takes me days and weeks of sustained work. Writing a book requires months of complete isolation over several years. My book, *Arab Intellectuals and the West*, took me six years to complete although its English text is no more than 150 pages long. I have spent many years of my life in complete solitude because of such work. My daily routine has not changed over the years: My day begins at 9AM and ends at 5PM, with a short break for a light lunch consisting of a sandwich that I prepare by myself and some fruits. The day's yield is usually no more than six or seven pages of a first draft, which I rewrite two or three times before I hand it over to be typed.

Charles Dickens says that genius is nothing but the capacity to take pains. If this is true, I must have touched the fringes of genius. The important thing, I believe, is to control oneself, to follow certain discipline, and to persevere in spite of everything. In my opinion, such discipline and the self-control it requires are more important than a natural capacity for creativity and inventiveness. In the final analysis, what we accomplish in life is the tangible, objective thing, not the intentions, the dreams, and the contemplations we harbor.

Most of the young Arab men I knew in Chicago had a large measure of sagacity and intelligence. Yet their intelligence was raw and not subject to intellectual discipline or conscious will. They may have been highly capable in practical matters and in relations with people on a personal level. But most proved failures in the intellectual disciplines their studies required. They were interested in people, not issues. They were quickly bored with the theoretical matters to which their American colleagues were inclined, and they preferred their own social gatherings where they could speak in Arabic on their favorite topics—stories, jokes, scandals.

It is not a coincidence that Arab society has not been able to produce a single thinker, scientist, or writer of international caliber since the nineteenth century awakening; for creativity cannot be acquired or imported, nor can it be studied abroad. It abides in the depths of the individual and it grows, develops, and flowers only if afforded a suitable environment. Otherwise, it vanishes and dies before anyone even learns of its existence. And it is society that offers it a suitable atmosphere by its ethics, its values, and its methods of education. If society is afraid of creativity and considers innovative forces a threat to its traditions and its heritage, it resorts to every means available to put an end to it, the most successful means being the repression of the individual from childhood— thereby shackling him intellectually and psychologically as an adult. How many a Shakespeare, an Einstein, a Marx has our society killed before the child reached adolescence?

-12-

I spent the winter in loneliness, enduring harsh living conditions and constant homesickness for my country and friends.

I got up daily at 6:30AM to the sound of hot water crackling in the pipes of the heating system. I took a bath, put on my clothes, went down to the cafeteria, and had a quick breakfast, then returned to my room. I put on my heavy boots and my thick winter overcoat; I wore wool earmuffs, wrapped a scarf around my neck, and put on my hat. I looked like a fat doll, and I could hardly move. Then I took the elevator downstairs and did not turn left or right.

When I opened the outer door of International House and went out into the dark world, I felt the poignancy of my loneliness as at no other time. The wind buffeted my face and tears flowed down my cheeks; I rubbed my tears with the edge of my scarf and walked, my head bent down and my body leaning forward against the wind.

After Bergstraesser's class ended at 9AM, I went to the library, read, and prepared the next day's lessons. The library was on the second floor of Swift Hall and was separated from Harbor Hall, where Bergstraesser's classroom and office were, by a tiny square in the middle of which stood a small church built in Gothic style. I walked to the church under the snow-laden branches of the trees, and I stood there for a few minutes listening to the bells, whose ringing reached me faintly across the piles of snow. I then hunched my shoulders and hastened to the library.

The library was my constant resort during the first semester. I spent hours on end there, moving among the racks of books, whose quantity and quality fascinated me. The number of books at the American University of Beirut did not exceed a few thousand all together in the various fields. Here at Chicago, the library of philosophy alone had tens of thousands of volumes. Nietzsche's complete works were available in the German original as well as in English and French translations. Next to them were shelves densely packed with books in various languages on Nietzsche's life and philosophy. Such was the case with all the rest of the philosophers, from Socrates to the modern ones.

I had lunch at a student cafeteria located in a building on 59th Street called Ida Neuss, which was not too far from the library. To this hour, whenever I sit to eat at a cafeteria, I remember Ida Neuss and the silent meals I ate there. My meal consisted of a plate of meat and vegetables, a salad, and dessert with a cup of coffee, and it cost me about fifty cents. I chose my food, put it on a tray, and sat at an unoccupied table. I opened a book and read while I ate. Male and female students sat sometimes at my table, but I did not stop reading unless one of them talked to me. After lunch, I went to class, if I had any scheduled, or I returned to the library where I spent my afternoon reading. At 5PM, I returned to International House and went up to my room to rest a little or write a few letters. Once a week, I took my laundry to the basement, where the washing machines were, and washed and sorted my clothes. At 6PM, I had supper at the cafeteria, went to the reading room, and read newspapers and magazines for half an hour, then went up to my room. I read until 11:30PM, then went to bed.

-13-

These months in Chicago were a new and hard experience for me. Before, I had always spent my time in the company of friends. I had always been busy in an atmosphere I knew and felt comfortable in. My time now was all mine, willy-nilly. I myself filled it with what I did and thought. I had become my own sole companion.

The loneliness imposed on me compelled me to deal with ideas and experiences I had never encountered before. There were no friends I could resort to when I was in difficulty, as I used to do in Beirut where we sat at Faysal's Restaurant or went for a walk or to the cinema. Here, there was no escape from myself and from what I was facing day and night. In Beirut, my social life filled all my leisure time and prevented me from reading or thinking much. Many a time I left the Lodge with a book under my arm that I planned to read sitting by the sea but of which I didn't read a single word. For it was usually only a few minutes before a friend passed by and stopped and sat next to me to talk; I closed the book without feeling any guilt. After a while, we went to Faysal's or to the Milk Bar to join a group of friends drinking coffee and telling jokes. I placed my book on the table and promised myself to read it in the evening or on the next day.

In Chicago, I had nothing but the library and my room—or the icy cold outdoors. I spent the whole first semester reading and studying for nine or ten hours a day. I sat to read and was not interrupted by anyone. And so, I learned serious reading, and I understood what Nietzsche meant by saying that reading was "the art of chewing, which only a cow knew well." Previously, reading to me had been something I wanted to finish with quickly in order to turn to other, more enjoyable things. In childhood, studying and eating were actually imposed on us, and they prevented us from playing and enjoying ourselves. In boarding school, too, the evening periods of study were imposed on us between 7 and 8:30PM and were a kind of daily detention during which we were virtually obliged to prepare our lessons for the next day. Being in one room all together was the only thing that reduced the burden of such imprisonment as it gave us the comfort of knowing that there was nobody playing outside and that we were not missing anything. This is why the method of reading that I had become accustomed to since early childhood was exactly contrary to the "chewing" to which Nietzsche referred. At school and later at the university, my friends and I were accustomed to read the same way we spoke, and to write the same way we read, namely, quickly and in loud oratorical tones and expressions. We were accustomed to look and to listen, not to understand, to analyze, to think.

I am reminded at this moment of 'Imran Shafiq (who was with me at prep school and later in the freshman class) and I see him sitting on his bed "to study": he would turn page after page while deeply immersed in daydreaming. On reaching the last page of the day's assigned reading, he would close the book and jump off the bed saying, "I finished studying," and he would turn to other important matters such as making a cup of coffee on his electric heater, the likes of which nobody else owned in Thompson Hall, or he would go to visit friends in another room or else go out to the Milk Bar. We were all like 'Imran. His aim (and ours too) was to escape from the burden of authority—from studying and reading. He did not do that by frank rejection or a clear encounter, but rather by subterfuge and cunning. The custom of "looking" at the book instead of reading it and of memorizing the lesson instead of understanding it was the simple result of the authoritative method of instruction we had grown up with.

I don't remember all the books I read in those first months in Chicago. Most had to do with my courses: Nietzsche, Aristotle, Burkhardt, William James, Charles Peirce, Kierkegaard. Yet after some time, I grew tired of continuous reading, and I began to spend longer periods in the lounge at International House and at the lunch table with the other students at Ida Neuss. But I always returned to my books.

Gradually, the book for me turned into a living thing, an intimate friend, a vital necessity. I found I was conversing with the book through its printed pages. Listening alone was not sufficient. I learned to reread whole passages, as though I was asking the author to repeat what he had said. I began to search for meanings that might have escaped me, which I wasn't used to doing. Having a vague idea was no longer enough for me. I began to make an effort to grasp the whole meaning and to insist on full clarity.

Hidden shackles that fettered my mind began to fall off. The darkness of many years began to disperse. My way of seeing things changed, not only regarding the content but also methods of understanding and analysis. It became possible for me (perhaps for the first time) to see matters from various viewpoints and in the light of different criteria and values. I suddenly felt I had penetrated an intellectual barrier that had prevented me from seeing things as they really were. It became possible for me to see my social self (perhaps for the first time also) from the "outside" and with an increasingly objective spirit.

-14-

Finally, spring arrived and my life was turned upside down.

On my birthday in April, I received my transcripts for the winter semester and they were utterly satisfying. A heavy burden was removed from my chest; I regained my self-confidence.

I began going less to the library and spending whole evenings in the lounge with my American and Arab fellow students. I went out with them to the Crazy Spoon Café and the bars on 55th Street for beer.

One weekend, I went to the Beehive for the first time. It was a small bar on 55th Street famous for its jazz music. I was in the company of an American friend and two girls living at International House like us. After we had had a few glasses of beer, I felt urgently I had to go to the men's room. But bashfulness prevented me, so I sat there repressing myself and not knowing what to do. A while later, the girl with me got up and said, rubbing the lower part of her abdomen, "It's the beer! It has to find its way out."

I blushed with embarrassment as I stood up to let her pass by me. Seizing the opportunity, I in turn went to the men's room. While there, a young American man who stood beside me at the urinal turned to me after undoing the buttons of his trousers and said, his face joyous, "This indeed is happiness itself, isn't that so?"

That was exactly my feeling, too, so I got rid of the heavy pressure and experienced the joy that made me love the whole world.

From that day on, when nature called, I no longer hesitated to ask frankly, "Where's the lavatory?"

-15-

In spring, a strong relationship developed between a colleague at the philosophy department and me. She lived at International House and our relationship soon developed into love. She hailed from California and was of Norwegian descent. Her name was Carol. I met with her a few times outside the classroom, and we had lunch together once or twice at Ida Neuss. I told her about Bergstraesser's course, and she began to attend it. One day, and it was a Saturday, I invited her out to an evening with me as well as Rashid and his girlfriend. She accepted the invitation, and that was the beginning of our relationship.

Rashid, his girlfriend, and I waited for her in the lounge. Then I saw her from a distance as, slow and unhurried, she came down the stairs. I hardly recognized her. Until then, I had only seen her in old, unattractive clothes: a worn-out sweater, a large wool skirt, bobby socks, and low-heeled shoes. Now, she was wearing a close-fitting white dress, high-heeled shoes, an expensive fur coat, and a small matching fur hat; she wore dark-red lipstick. She was indeed very attractive. The young men sitting around us followed her with their eyes. As for me, I was a little embarrassed, but also proud. We went out of the lounge, followed by the gaze of everyone in the room.

Rashid's girlfriend made it a condition that we take the train or a taxi, because she didn't have confidence in his driving, especially at night. But Carol volunteered to drive Rashid's used Oldsmobile, and I sat in the front seat next to her, while Rashid and his girlfriend sat in the back. That was the first time I went downtown. Carol drove us there on the Outer Drive along the lake. The skyscrapers loomed in the distance above the city lights as the dark lake water stretched out on our right. I looked at Carol holding the steering wheel, her beautiful profile clear in the dark. She was the first American girl I fell in love with. She was 20 and I, 21.

Rashid led us to a café called the High Hat, located in the most magnificent hotel in Chicago. We sat at a small table with a candle in the middle. The waiter lit the candle and stood by to take our order. Carol ordered whiskey and I, a Tom Collins (it was the only cocktail whose name I remembered at that moment). I drank it quickly and asked for another. After my long loneliness, I now felt greatly exhilarated: I talked to Carol without stop. All the ideas accumulating in my mind in the recent months about Nietzsche, Kierkegaard, and Dostoevsky flowed on my tongue in a current of words. Carol looked at me with her green eyes and did not say much except to ask a question or encourage me to go on. And I drank a third Tom Collins.

We stayed at the café until two in the morning. On our way back, we stopped at the Crazy Spoon for coffee. When we returned to International House, it was about four o'clock. On the next day, I woke up at noon and called Carol on the telephone to ask her to meet me at the cafeteria. We spent the remainder of Sunday together. In the evening, we went to the movies. I had not kissed her nor touched her all those days, and I think she found that strange and perhaps even regarded it as a bad omen. But she was reassured and regained her cheerfulness when I took her in my arms, one warm evening in the park.

-16-

Carol and springtime changed my way of life. I continued to study, to read, and to attend seminars and lectures according to my earlier program, but I remained moderate with regard to evening parties, going to cafés, and drinking, not on account of will power—will power is hardly a deterrent in most matters—but for two reasons: my limited funds and my growing intellectual thirst.

Despite the financial difficulties that continued from then until my return to Beirut, this new phase of my life was happy and free from the loneliness and depression I had experienced during the winter. When I opened the door of International House in the morning, I began to be met by a pleasant spring breeze, and I walked to my class elatedly, greeting colleagues I met on the way and smiling at everybody. I began to sit in the cafeteria at tables crowded with students, with Carol at my side, and I took part in the conversation and told stories and jokes. It was the same trans-formation every Arab student underwent after the first months of loneliness following his arrival in the United States. What the movies and the magazines portrayed as American life was nothing but a myth. They presented American reality not as it actually was, but as Americans dreamed of it. Americans are like Arabs: They go to the movies not to see their life with all its hardship and bore-dom, but to escape from it to a beautiful world that Hollywood invents for them.

There is not a single Arab student who has not been disap-pointed on arriving in America. The first thing he discovers is that American girls are not all as beautiful as those appearing in the movies and magazines, and that it is difficult to reach those of them endowed with some beauty because competition for them is strong. Months pass by before he can become the boyfriend of a girl with an acceptable figure. I know young men from Arab coun-tries who have spent years in America without ever establishing an emotional connection or experiencing a sexual relationship.

Beauty in the United States—like experience, intelligence, and talent—is a commodity that can be sold and bought, not only in the moral sense but also in the material sense that imposes a particular way of life and work on a beautiful woman merely because she is beautiful. The most attractive female students I saw in Chicago were students at Northwestern University, near Chicago, and I was stunned to learn that some of them were employed as part-time dancers in a striptease café in Calumet City, a small town to the south of Chicago.

I still remember the first time I went to Calumet City in the company of Fawzi Kahhalu, Rashid, and an Iraqi student studying ancient history at the University of Chicago named 'Abd al-Qadir al-Yusuf. Fawzi was the eldest among us and was working as an engineer at one of the local engineering companies. He had a new Pontiac in which he would take us for a drive from time to time; he forbade us to smoke in it. One evening, Rashid, 'Abd al-Qadir, and I were sitting and talking in the lounge of International House when Fawzi entered and said, "Who wants to come with me and see something he's never seen in his life?"

Rashid asked, "And where is this great thing?"

"It doesn't matter. Are you coming or not?"

"We're coming, but tell us where to?"

"To the strip club in Calumet City."

I didn't know what a strip club was. So I asked Fawzi, and he laughed and said, "You don't know what a strip club is? Shame on you. Come on, young fellows. Let's go and show Hisham what a strip club is."

We went to his Pontiac with comfortable leather seats. We extinguished our cigarettes before getting in, and then drove southward to Calumet City, which was about twenty miles away.

Fawzi first took us to a small café that had a circular bar on which stood a little stage. The place was almost empty of clients, so we sat and ordered our four glasses of beer. Minutes later, a very beautiful girl appeared on the stage. Short-haired and slender, she was naked except for a cloth covering her loins and she began dancing to the music played by a band consisting of a pianist, a drummer, and a trombone player. We looked at her from our seats at the bar, and she looked down at us and smiled. When the music reached a climax, the girl whirled fast several times, then removed the little cloth on her loins and left the stage, her left hand hiding her vulva and her right hand waving the cloth. A short while later, another girl replaced her, just as beautiful, but wearing a long evening gown. The band began a new tune, and the girl began to walk slowly around the stage. She took off her clothes, piece by piece, beginning with her leather gloves. When she reached the bra, Fawzi could hardly contain himself and began to applaud and cheer enthusiastically. Rashid, 'Abd al-Qadir and I continued to watch without uttering a single sound. Finally, she took off her remaining clothes, except for a thin string on her loins. She danced in front of us, then she whirled as her colleague had done earlier, and she left the stage running as a red spotlight aimed at her buttocks.

We moved to a second café, then to a third, and saw variations on the same scene: beautiful girls taking off their clothes to a musical accompaniment, then running out of sight with red spotlights on their posteriors. I particularly remember one, perhaps the youngest, who had blond hair and fair skin. She came on stage wearing an American Indian headdress and began to dance an Indian dance, shouting every now and then. She took off her clothes, piece by piece, until she was wearing only a bra. She unfastened it from behind her back and her round breasts appeared, a red ribbon suspended from each of her nipples. Suddenly, she began to gyrate to the music, and the two ribbons on her breasts spun as though they were airplane propellers.

The barman informed us that all the girls were students at Northwestern University and that they worked at Calumet City entertainment centers a few hours a week, earning more than they could have from any job at the university. I asked him about the girl in the Indian costume, and he told me that she was from Houston, Texas, and that she was eighteen years old.

Since I began writing these pages, my dreams have teemed with past events, and memories like this one, which I thought time had effaced, have returned to me.

-17-

As of this writing, about 30 years have passed since I began living in the United States. During this period, no relation that I would call friendship has developed between an American man and me—in the manner we understand friendship in Arab society. The reasons for this are cultural and social. First, friendship among men in American society is different from friendship in our society. Second, I have always preferred the companionship of American women to that of American men, not for sexual or emotional reasons, but because I have found them to have more intelligence, vitality, and cheer. In the company of an American woman, I feel a pleasure and satisfaction that I never feel in the presence of an American man. Of course, there are exceptions. And I would like here to speak about one of these exceptions, Marshall Hodgson, who was a fellow student with me at the University of Chicago and who became a professor of Islamic history there, then died of an incurable disease.

I came to know Marshall while he was working on his doctorate in the history of Islamic civilization. He used to spend most of his time at the library of the Oriental Institute, where I too often went to read. Because he was a Quaker, he abstained from alcohol, smoking, and meat.

Marshall used to eat his lunch every day on the steps of the library. It consisted usually of a cheese sandwich with an apple or orange, and he continued to read as he ate it. I met him for the first time on the steps of the library. He asked me about my field of specialization, and we talked. Our friendship became stronger as the days went by. I began to buy a roast-beef or ham sandwich every day with some kind of fruit or dessert, and I started eating my lunches on the steps with him.

One day, Marshall asked whether I did any kind of sport. I said I swam in the summer. He said, "We need to exercise. Sitting down all day long is bad for one's health and weakens the circulation. What do you think of joining the university swimming pool?"

I agreed with his proposal enthusiastically, and we went on the spot to the university gymnasium, which was not more than fifty meters away from the Oriental Institute. The staff member there gave each of us a key and a small locker for our belongings, and showed us where the swimming pool was. It was almost empty, and he told us that it remained empty most days and that we could swim any time we wanted. Since then, I began going to the library of the Oriental Institute three times a week. I read until lunch time, then I ate my lunch with Marshall on the steps. Afterward, we both went to the gymnasium and swam, then returned to the library to study until five o'clock. Marshall was writing his dissertation on the Isma'ili movement and used to tell me about the difficulties he was facing in his research and the method he was following. He used to ask me about the meaning of certain religious terms. His reading knowledge of Arabic was excellent, although he could not speak Arabic fluently.

Marshall was a quiet and gentle person who never uttered an unseemly word. He was deeply religious but not a fanatic. He disliked violence and believed in Gandhi's pacifism. Despite dissimilar qualities in our characters and in our ways of seeing things, our friendship grew quickly. During all that time, I met with Marshall in two places only: on the steps of the library at the Oriental Institute and in the gymnasium, and I don't remember ever meeting elsewhere.

Several years later, Marshall graduated with distinction and was appointed as a professor at the university; he became the chairman of the Committee on Social Thought after Neef's retirement. In that period, he finished his famous book, *Venture of Islam* (in three volumes), which was the culmination of his twenty years of studies in Islamic civilization. The book was published a few months after his death. I consider it the most important book on Islamic history written in the twentieth century.

Relations between us were cut off after I left Chicago in 1951. We did not meet again until 1963, when I returned to Chicago to attend a conference on the political system in Lebanon. I saw him on the Midway by coincidence. I had gone outdoors for some fresh air after a session full of trivialities that had lasted most of the afternoon and in which Dr. Malik had participated in his usual manner. A voice called me in the street, so I stopped, turned toward it, and saw a person crossing the street and waving his hand to me. I did not recognize him at first and thought he was waving to someone else. He called me again, and I recognized him: it was Marshall Hodgson. We shook hands warmly and talked for a moment. Then I asked whether he still swam in the gymnasium, and he said, "Every day and at the same time."

"And the cheese sandwich?" I asked.

"Every day also, but in my office rather than on the library steps."

"With an apple?"

"With an apple or an orange. And you, how are you? Do you swim in Washington? Your health seems to be fine."

There was a marked change in his appearance, for he had lost weight, and his hair had turned gray. He looked as though he was several years older than I was. Only his eyes behind his glasses remained as I remembered them—meek and dreamy. He said he was on his way to an appointment, and we parted on the understanding that we would meet again before I returned to Washington. But we did not meet. A short while later, I heard that his twin daughters were suffering from an incurable disease, and he patiently bore the agonizing pains it dealt him, until death relieved him.

-18-

Death touched my life at different times. It snatched away friends of mine in childhood. In the early days of my youth, it seized my dearest friends, one after another. Then it wrested away Sa'adah.

I used to feel it was going to snatch me early. When I turned 30, I was convinced that my life was about to end. At 35, I strongly believed that what remained of it was only a few years. When I turned 40, I was sure that death was inevitably around the corner, for it was around this age that Kierkegaard had died (43), and Sa'adah (45), and Camus (47). But death did not come. And a few days ago, I celebrated my 49th birthday. The fifties will be upon me soon. I have come to believe that death has overlooked me, and that is why I don't expect it any more. I have also come to believe that the future stretches before me indefinitely. The prospect of an end to my life no longer causes a tragic feeling in my soul.

I look in the mirror and see my face as I have always known it—unchanged. I do not see the changes until I look at the faces of the friends of my boyhood or at those of my former students. Yesterday, in the elevator I saw one of my first students at Georgetown. I had not seen him since he graduated in the early 1960s. He was handsome then and in the prime of life. Now, he is a middle-aged man with wrinkles on his face. How does he think I look, I wonder?

I feel the change in another way. When girls pass by me in the street, they do not see me. My eyes meet theirs, but I do not see any sign that they feel I exist. The magic current has been cut off, the burning fire has been extinguished.

And so I admit that my youth has come to an end.

-19-

I was nine years old when, for the first time, I experienced the bitterness of the death of a dear one. An intimate friend of mine in Jaffa named Nicola Tadros, who was a student with me at the Friends' Boys School in Ramallah, was stolen away by death. A few years later, death took another friend, Subhi Qa'war, who hailed from Nazareth.

One day, Nicola had a headache as we were playing. The prefect advised him to go to the infirmary to see the doctor, and we continued to play. After supper, we learned that Nicola was kept at the infirmary; Subhi and I went to visit him, but the nurse refused to let us see him. The next day, he was taken to the hospital in an ambulance, and a few days later the principal announced that Nicola Tadros had passed away.

Nicola, like me, was nine years old. His favorite dish was white beans and rice, and when it was served to us in the school refectory, he ate it all up and swept his plate clean with bread. I walked in his funeral procession in Jaffa: that was the first funeral procession I ever walked in. I still remember the cemetery: overlooking the blue sea, it was full of poplar trees and marble statues; the women and children walked very slowly; Nicola's cousin, Marius, who was our schoolmate at the Friends', walked behind the coffin with tears flowing down his cheeks.

Three images returned to me with clarity as I related stories of that period of my life to my daughter Layla, who is now six years old. Every night before she sleeps, Layla insists that I tell her about my school life and my adventures with my friend "Nadim," the name she made up for Nicola. So I told her about Nadim's sickness, his sudden death, and his funeral. This affected her deeply, and so she demanded that I talk to her about Nadim every night. Nadim (i.e., Nicola) became an important person in her life because of his death. And thus Nicola returned to life every evening, and so did all my schoolmates at the Friends' Boys School as I told Layla about memories of that period of my life. She participated in this way in my childhood and learned that my little friends were not much older than she was. Through imagination, she lived the life I had lived in Ramallah 40 years ago.

Death snatched Subhi away a few years later. We used to sit side by side in the classroom, and we competed with each other for the attention of our mathematics and sports teacher, who was a Lebanese man named Tanios Bikh'azi. Mr. Bikh'azi held a special place among us for two reasons: first, because he was a sportsman, and secondly, because he smoked secretly. Smoking at the Friends' was considered an evil act as hideous as drinking alcohol. That is why he won our admiration. Mr. Bikh'azi used to give Subhi more attention than he gave me, and his favoritism aroused my jealousy and made me increase my efforts to get his attention. One day, I tried to draw his attention to me in class by answering a question he had addressed to Subhi but which my friend could not answer quickly. The teacher tried to shut me up, but I continued answering the question, so he interrupted me angrily and asked me to leave the classroom.

Utterly crushed, I rose to my feet. I had expected to win his admiration but, instead, he had kicked me out of the classroom in front of Subhi and my other classmates. I walked to the door scarcely able to see my way. I went out disconcerted, seeking a place to hide and wishing that the earth would swallow me up and that I would vanish. That is how I remember my first love for a person other than my father.

In that year (1938), my family moved to Beirut and my father registered me as a student at the prep school attached to the American University. On the first day of school, I was greatly surprised to see Subhi enter the classroom. I called to him, he sat in the seat next to me, and our friendship was renewed.

Subhi died in the summer holidays of 1943. I was in Jaffa preparing to go to 'Akka when I heard of his death. A friend of mine, who was a student with us at the Friends' School and whose name I don't recall, conveyed the news to me. I was on my way to Alhambra Cinema when I met this friend near City Hall at the beginning of Jamal Pasha Street.

"Have you heard the news about Subhi?"

"Subhi who?"

"Subhi Qa'war."

"What about him?"

"Subhi died."

I experienced the feeling of a passenger in an airplane as it falls into an air pocket.

"How did he die?"

"From sunstroke."

He was on a mountain-climbing trip to Mount Sinnin with a number of his friends. It appears that he lost his hat on the way, and was thus exposed to the sun. When he reached the top of the mountain, he felt dizzy and couldn't walk. His friends carried him to Baskinta. They then drove him to the University Hospital in Beirut. But he soon departed this life.

-20-

A few years ago, another dear friend of mine named Majid Sa'id died, here in the United States. Majid was originally from a small village near Ramallah. He was the first young Arab man whose acquaintance I made at Georgetown University when I joined its faculty in 1953. He taught linguistics at that time. After he obtained his doctorate, he was appointed to teach Arabic at Princeton University. He got married and had two daughters. From time to time, I visited him in Princeton, and he came over to Washington to visit me. In the spring of 1966, I was invited to take part in a conference at Princeton, organized by Hanna Mikha'il, who taught there at the time. As soon as I arrived, I got in touch with Hanna and asked him about Majid. He told me that Majid was sick and hospitalized and that the doctors knew neither the cause nor the nature of the disease. He also said he would pick me up so that we could go together to visit him. As the hospital was near my hotel, we went on foot. We climbed the stairs to Majid's room, and Hanna opened the door. We saw Majid sitting up in bed, propped up on four or five pillows and reading a newspaper. When he saw us, a big smile shone all over his face. He said he would leave the hospital within a few days and that he could complain of absolutely nothing but a headache now and then, accompanied by dizziness. After I returned to Washington, I called Majid at home, confident that he would be back there. His wife told me that Majid's disease had taken a turn for the worse and that he had been transferred to a hospital in New York. She gave me his telephone number at the hospital. I called him immediately and a faint voice answered. I thought at first that it was the result of bad connection, but it was Majid's voice. He was in such a weak state that he was not allowed to speak much. I said goodbye and promised to call the next day.

The next day his voice was stronger and his speech clearer. He told me that the doctors were not sure of the nature of his disease. They had given him different drugs, some of which were tranquilizers that impaired his ability to speak. He appeared to be in good psychological condition, so I was reassured and told him that Joseph Salamah and Yusuf al-Khal were in New York and would visit him shortly. We agreed that I would call him a few days later. I contacted Yusuf in New York on the spot (he knew Majid very well), and I asked him to go with Joseph to visit him and ask the doctor responsible about his condition.

A few hours later, Joseph Salamah called me and reported that Majid had leukemia and that there was no hope of a cure for him. I had expected that.

Majid's struggle with death continued for several weeks. I spoke with him on the phone once a week, the last time in May 1966 from Nags Head on the North Carolina shore, where I was spending the summer with my wife. I called him from a telephone booth by the roadside. There was a violent storm in the region on that day, and Majid's voice was faint, as thunder pealed now and then and overwhelmed it. He said that his health was constantly improving and that everything was fine. It was the last time I heard his voice. He departed this life a week later, after the tranquilizers had become ineffective in killing his pain. One of those who visited him at the hospital before he died told me that he had lost so much weight that he had shrunk to the size of a child. His body before burial was exposed at a funeral home in Princeton in accordance with his wife's wishes so that his friends could see him for the last time. But I refused to see him in that condition. We carried Majid's coffin and walked to the cemetery behind the Catholic church in the center of town, where we interred him.

-21-

By the end of that first spring semester at Chicago, I had spent all that remained of my money, except for a $20 balance in my bank account. Fortunately, I was granted sufficient financial aid by the university to pay my fees and the rent for my room at International House. But I was in need of a job to pay for food and my other daily expenses. I looked for a job, and I economized as much as possible. I started eating my breakfast in my room, making myself a sandwich to eat at lunch time, and having only the evening meal at the cafeteria. On the day that I withdrew the remainder of my balance at the bank, I was informed by the university employment office that there was an opening at one of the meatpacking companies. I went there immediately with Carol. It was in one of the dirtiest neighborhoods of Chicago, where pigs and cows were slaughtered by machines, cut into pieces, and packed in cans, nothing remaining of them but their hides and their feet. Even these were washed and sold. The awful smell increased as we approached the factory. I entered the personnel office hesitantly, followed by Carol, and carrying a letter I was given by the woman who managed the university employment office. The man looked at the letter, then he looked up at me and said, "What's your weight?"

I answered, "One hundred and thirty pounds."

"Can you carry a weight of seventy pounds?"

"I don't know. Perhaps."

The job consisted of carrying large pieces of pork and beef, between fifty and seventy pounds each, from the place where they were cut to the inside of the refrigerators, where the temperature was twenty below zero. I realized on the spot that I would be unable to do this job.

Before I responded, the man said, "Sorry, I don't think you can do this job."

We returned to International House without regret. On the next morning, I went to the university employment office and informed the manager about what had happened at the factory. She took my card, looked in the file, and said smilingly, "You're lucky. A vacancy has opened up today at the university, and I don't think the job requires great strength."

The job was at the Faculty Club, which I knew well, for I had eaten my lunch there several times in the company of Bergstraesser. The woman responsible for managing the club received me in her magnificent office and explained my duties. It became clear to me that my job was to be a porter. I had to wear a shirt like those worn by waiters, and wait for guests in the reception hall in order to carry their luggage to their rooms. She said, "When you carry a suitcase to the room, open the curtain and the windows, and stand by the door for a moment saying, 'Will this be all, sir?' If the guest gives you a tip, thank him and leave. If he doesn't, don't put out your hand or say anything else. Thank him respectfully and leave."

Lunch time had arrived, so the manager led me to the kitchen and made me sit at a round table, where I had lunch with some other employees. I was very sad. "Me? A porter?" I controlled myself. On the next day, I did not go to work.

Finally, I got a satisfactory job at the university library. I was appointed as a guard to search those leaving the library to be sure they hadn't stolen any books. I worked fifteen hours per week, scheduled in a way to agree with my academic program: on weekdays, the evening hours were from 7 to 10PM, the library closing time; on Saturday, I worked from 2 to 5 in the afternoon. At those times, the library was almost empty. I sat at my desk at the entrance, reading and studying most of the time. When I was tired of reading, I talked to my colleagues, the girls who worked in the circulation department, and they left their work and sat with me. I was paid $15 a week, excluding income tax, and the amount was sufficient to meet all my needs. Thus did I manage to solve my financial crisis, and my life went on well, until the situation in Palestine grew worse.

-22-

That was at the beginning of spring. Until then, everyone expected an Arab victory in Palestine in spite of the "setbacks" suffered by Palestinian cities and villages. After supper, the Arab students would gather in the lounge at International House and analyze the news. The Egyptian students treated the subject more cheerfully than the others. They were not so directly involved (the Egyptian forces had not yet entered Palestine); for that reason, they were quickly bored by conversation on this topic and began to joke, laugh, and talk on other topics.

I still felt pity for the Jews in Palestine. I had not forgotten the event related to me by Kamil in 'Akka before I left. I wished the Arabs would not be harsh with them. It was enough to stop them, I thought. It did not occur to me that things would be the other way around, that we would be the victims and they the harsh victors.

At the end of March, I began to read the *New York Times* every day. It arrived by 11AM and provided details concerning daily events, as reported by the two correspondents Dana Adam Smith and Gene Carrigan.

In April I began to be afraid. It was clear that the Jews were in an offensive position. The Arab withdrawals were not merely tactical. While the Jewish forces possessed armored cars and guns and an organized military leadership, the Arab situation was fragmented and in a state of disarray and falling back. The traditional leaders were in conflict with one another, and the military forces, foremost the Deliverance Army, were fighting haphazardly, without coordination or cooperation among factions.

In his memoirs, Fawzi al-Qawuqji says that the Deliverance Army lacked men and ammunition and that its communications were in a state of permanent chaos. When ammunition was depleted and he asked the leadership in Damascus for replenishment, he received promises but never any ammunition. He was, therefore, obliged to withdraw from one position after another.

The stage was set for tragedy. I was sure of that as I followed, daily, the developments reported in the *New York Times*.

April was the decisive month.

On April 6, the Jews penetrated the siege laid by the Arabs around Jerusalem, and a convoy carrying provisions and ammunition entered the city. On the next day, the Jews occupied the villages of Khalda and Dayr Muhsin on the road to Jerusalem.

On April 8, 'Abd al-Qadir al-Husayni was martyred at al-Qastal, and on April 21 the Jews attacked the village of Dayr Yasin and destroyed it utterly (there was no mention of the massacre in the *New York Times*).

On April 12, the Zionist Council held a general meeting in Tel

Aviv and decided on May 16, 1948, to establish an independent Jewish state on the soil of Palestine.

On April 19, the town of Tiberias fell, and on the 22nd it was followed by Haifa. At the end of April, Jaffa fell.

Dana Smith in Tel Aviv cabled the following on May 1:

> The Star of David fluttered today above the Manshiyya Quarter in Jaffa when the Haganah forces, in the name of the State of Israel, received the positions which the forces of the Irgun Zvai Leumi had occupied after violent fighting lasting four days. The British authorities are now helping the inhabitants of Jaffa to evacuate by sea on two ships anchored in its port.

On May 2, he sent the following cable:

> With signs of visible exhaustion on his face, the leader of the Irgun forces said as he shook hands with the Haganah officer who had come to receive the command of the position occupied earlier by the Irgun forces in Jaffa: "I hand over to you a land for which we paid a high price. So don't give it up easily."
>
> The Haganah officer replied: "We shall never give up the honor of defending it."
>
> This conversation took place in one of the destroyed buildings surrounded by machine guns and heavy artillery, as the enemy lurked behind the debris on the other side of the street, where the Mediterranean Sea loomed with its greenish blue color at a distance of one hundred yards.
>
> In the street behind the Hasan Bey Mosque, which Arab snipers used in order to fire on Tel Aviv, dead bodies were strewn on the ground. And on the minaret, the flag of the Jewish State fluttered beside the white flag of surrender which the Arabs had hoisted.

The Manshiyya Quarter... the Hasan Bey Mosque. Not far from the mosque, at a distance of two blocks, lived Shaykh 'Abbas Baydas, a friend of my father's, who was the grandfather of Baydas Baydas and his brother Birjis, both schoolmates of mine at the Friends' Boys School.

Our house was not very far from theirs. We had moved to it when I was in the third grade, and it was next to the "greenish blue" sea.

I remember the sea of Jaffa well. It is the sea of my childhood. I can smell it at this very moment, I can taste its salty taste, I can feel its breeze on my face…. Its color was truly greenish blue when it was calm. But in stormy weather, it became dark gray. I learned to swim it, and I swallowed large quantities of its water. In the summer, early in the morning, my older brothers Nizam and Nazim ran to the shore to swim with the children of the Yusuf Talib family, our neighbors. I followed them despite my mother's threats and warnings. We used to go out of the door and directly to the sea. The older boys used to run to the waves, jump over them and swim through them until they reached calm water. I followed them and tasted the salt in my throat. I coughed and my nose was filled with the scent of the sea and my eyes with tears. I looked around and saw the port of Jaffa with the old city rising behind it, protruding into the sea. Today it is called the "city of artists and tourists." To the right, I saw the shore stretching toward Tel Aviv.

Our home was on the second floor, above that of Yusuf Talib and contiguous with that of Malas. It overlooked the main street of the Manshiyya Quarter. The police department and the Mughrabi pharmacy were not very far from it. On the opposite side, there was a small shop from which I used to buy a Cadbury chocolate bar or Oh Boy chewing gum for half a piaster.

On the seaside, at the very edge of the shore, stood the Rawda School, in which I was enrolled before I was transferred to the English School on Tamimi Street. I was four or five years old when I moved to the English School at the insistence of my mother, who wanted me to have a modern upbringing, i.e., at the hands of the female English teachers. I used to go to school in the company of my maternal aunt Ni'mat, who was then a girl of twelve or thirteen and a student in the preparatory section of the same school. She came to our house daily at half past seven in the morning, riding in a buggy which took us both to school and returned us home in the afternoon. One day, an accident happened on the way, so we had to stop. I looked out from the buggy and saw a man lying on the ground with blood flowing from his head. That was the first time I ever saw blood. It was dark red and became dark brown as it mixed with the soil. People shouted and shoved one another until the police came and traffic resumed its movement.

I remember the day on which the Manshiyya bus line was inaugurated. Its buses were especially made for the narrow streets of the Manshiyya Quarter. The fare was half a piaster, and at the beginning there were no designated bus stops on the way. People who wanted a ride stood anywhere on the side of the road and signaled to the driver with a coin in their hands. He often did not stop, when he was in a hurry; or he stopped to pick up everyone he met, when he had extra time. He was sometimes invited by friends for a cup of coffee; then he might stop the bus, get off, and sit at the café while his passengers waited.

The horse-drawn carriage, in those days, was like a taxi. My father never rode the bus because of his eminent social position, so when he hired a carriage, he sometimes permitted me to sit by the driver—and that gave me great happiness.

The neighborhood children used to run behind the carriage and cling to its rear. Passersby shouted, "Strike your rear," and he would strike the rear of the carriage with his whip, sometimes hitting his target and causing those clinging to cry with pain and jump off, and sometimes missing so that they remained clinging all the way to the end of the street. Horses often had a call of nature during the trip: they raised their tails, not very far from the driver's seat, and let out round balls that fell like bombs on the ground. Whenever I now smell the sweet smell of horse dung, memories and images of the Manshiyya come to my mind.

I heard that the military occupation of the Manshiyya was complete within a few days and that the remaining inhabitants of Jaffa left the city in 24 hours, and that the Jews then declared it "an open city."

-23-

I sat in the Midway every day, I read the details of the catastrophe, and my despair grew worse. My relatives had become refugees, my people were now without a homeland, and I was homeless.

Only my belief in the Party saved me from this state of despair. I sincerely believed that the Party would liberate Palestine and remove the shame that had befallen us. I continued to believe this

until Sa'adah was assassinated and the Party was crushed in
Lebanon, until the Arab states signed armistice agreements with
Israel in 1949.

-24-

More than six months had passed since my arrival in Chicago. I
had seen almost nothing of this vast country, other than this one
city, or rather some of its suburbs. I had no desire to see anything.
I determined to leave the city and return to my homeland. My
heart and mind were there. What was happening there was the
focus of all my concerns. Every passing day brought the moment
of return nearer. I did not go back on the decision I had made on
the day of my arrival. I would stop at the master's degree; I did not
want a doctorate. What would I need it for, now? I would complete
my basic requirements this term, the summer term, and I would
write my thesis during the next term. Before the beginning of the
Christmas holidays, I would sit for the final examinations. If everything went without a hitch, I would graduate before the end of the
year and be able to return home at the beginning of 1949.

I began the summer term with determination and confidence.
I needed nine credits only, that is, three more courses. For the first
time during registration, I was not worried about the payment of
fees. In addition to the three courses, I registered for a course
offered by a professor in the philosophy department named T. F.
Smith, and its subject was the British philosopher T. H. Green's
book *Ethics*.

Smith's class met at 2PM, when the heat was at its worst. In
those days, there was no air conditioning at the university.
Chicago's summer was hot and humid, especially in the afternoon.
I entered the classroom on the first day expecting the students to
be grumbling as they had at the American University in Beirut
when the summer season approached. In Beirut, we insisted that
the professor let us go out in the open air and sit in the shade of a
tree overlooking the sea, and we spent the class hour lying on the
ground lost in daydreams. Here, I found the students fully alert;
there were about twenty of them.

Professor Smith was 50 years old and wore an elegant summer
suit and a matching tie. He was an interesting lecturer who drew

the attention of his audience with his voice and the style of his delivery. The students followed his words with great attention and took notes in notebooks drenched with sweat. Now and then, I turned around to see if anyone was yawning, but they were all writing or listening carefully.

Before going to Professor Smith's class, I usually had a sandwich with Marshall then walked a little in the Midway until 2PM. In the afternoons when I was free, I went at noon to see Carol in the library and we walked together to the supermarket to buy what we needed to make a sandwich, then we went to Stony Island Park, which was a public park near the lake, full of trees and flowers, deserted at that time of day. We sat in the shade of a tree and ate our food in complete solitude.

On very hot days, we went to the lake shore, took off our clothes and lay down on the sand. Very few people swim in Lake Michigan because it is too cold, but I didn't know that. On our first trip to the lake shore, the temperature was above 90° Fahrenheit. When we got there, I quickly took off my shirt and pants—I had my swimming trunks on already—and I ran toward the water. I heard Carol calling out to me, "Wait, don't step into the water."

But I didn't stop. As we used to do in Beirut, I dashed into the water until it reached my waist. Then I stopped. I felt that the lower part of my body had become frozen, and I lost the ability to move. Nobody was swimming. Everyone was sitting on the shore. I tried to move my feet but could not. I was sure I had been struck with paralysis. I saw Carol standing at the edge of the lake, trying hard not to laugh, in my pain I looked ridiculous. Finally, I forced myself to move toward the shore, which was no more than a few yards away. Carol rubbed my feet and legs with the towel until I began to feel the blood running again in my veins. That was the first and the last time I ever swam in Lake Michigan.

-25-

In June, the first armistice in Palestine was declared. Several months had passed since I had heard from my family.

The last I had heard was that my mother and younger brother Khalid were in 'Akka at my grandfather's. When the Jews later attacked the city, all my relatives escaped to Beirut and stayed with

Khayriyya Hanim, a woman related to my grandmother, who lived in a small apartment in Ras Beirut near the Shawran Hill. They later moved to a small apartment in the Basta Quarter, on the tramway line. A few months later, my brother Khalid died and then my grandfather. Of those who had gone to Beirut, only the women survived: my mother, my grandmother, my great aunt (my grandfather's sister), and my two maternal aunts.

My father and elder brother Nizam were in Jaffa when the Jews attacked it. They escaped to Nablus (on the West Bank), my father's birthplace, and they lived there for a few months before moving to Amman, where they stayed with my uncle Shakib, who had been living there before the war.

-26-

At first, I didn't realize that what happened to us in Palestine was a blow different from all our previous afflictions. All our past had been a chain of misfortunes. But misfortunes came and dissipated, and our lives continued essentially unchanged. Now, however, our very roots were torn out. We had lost the land in which our lives had been rooted.

When al-Qassam's rebellion broke out in 1936, I was a nine-year-old student at the Friends' School. Travel was prohibited at night, and markets were closed day and night. But at the Friends' School, everything was available. They gave us the usual afternoon sandwich consisting of fresh bread, oil, and thyme; and sometimes molasses and tahini; or yogurt spread, which was very sour. During the Christmas and the spring holidays, I used to return to Jaffa, where Flash Gordon movies were shown serially at the Alhambra Cinema. I spent the spring and the summer vacations in 'Akka, where at sunset we used to see the British squads leave the Mafjar Camp on their way to Safad and to Galillee villages. They generally consisted of an armored car or two, followed by a busload of soldiers. On the top of the bus, two soldiers would lie down behind the Bren gun fixed to the roof. The sight of soldiers, especially the two on top of the bus, was extremely exciting, and we used to imitate them in our games on top of a junked car in front of Kamil and Akram's house.

During the 1936 rebellion, we truly lacked nothing. Well-to-do families were far from danger's way. Only the peasants and the deprived classes fought and suffered, and they paid the price of the rebellion. The educated people and the gentlemen, on the other hand, followed the news of the rebellion in *Falastin* and *Al-Difa'*, two popular newspapers. We heard that so-and-so had been killed, a house had been blown up, a rebel had been sentenced to death, and we cursed the English. But our life continued to follow its normal pattern.

In the summer of 1938, an event occurred that had a great effect on the course of my life. An unknown person attempted to assassinate 'Umar al-Bitar, an intimate friend of my father's and one of the leaders of the opposition in Palestine. 'Umar al-Bitar was one of those who continued to wear the fez, thus challenging the rebels.

When my mother heard the news, she began to pack. "We must leave immediately. Your father's turn is coming."

In the morning, Abu Zaki and his wife went to Lebanon by car. On the next day, my father, my mother, and I followed them. At 'Aley, Abu Zaki and my father put on the fez and went to the coffee house overlooking Beirut. They sat at a small, round table and began to smoke their hubble-bubble pipes with pleasure and in silence as though they were saying: the world is okay!

At the end of the summer, we went down to Beirut, and my father rented a small apartment near the lighthouse, at the end of the tramway line. He enrolled me at the Preparatory School for the American University. In the following year, my father and mother returned to Jaffa, and I became a boarder at school, thus remaining in Beirut until I graduated from the American University in 1947. During this period, I returned to Palestine only sporadically, for some of the school holidays.

The Second World War did not affect my life very much. Sugar changed color, white bread became dark, lights at night were blue and dim. Otherwise, nothing worth mentioning happened. I saw very little of the war. In the summer of 1941, from the roof of my grandfather's house in 'Akka, I watched little Italian airplanes bomb the oil refineries near Haifa and small plumes of smoke rise in the sky, and then the air raid ended. Once, the air raid sirens went off in Beirut, and we rushed to the shelters in the football playground. We saw two airplanes at a great height, and Mr. As'ad, our physics teacher, said they were German. That was the first and last time we ever went to the bomb shelter.

In the summer of 1941, the Allies occupied Syria and Lebanon. I was in 'Akka at the time, swimming and fishing and riding bicycles with Kamil and Akram. When I returned to Beirut toward the end of September, I found nothing changed, except that there were many British soldiers about and a greater variety of French, American, and British movies.

When the 1948 disaster took place, I was only slightly affected by it. But I was dealt a direct and heavy blow in 1949, when the Party was destroyed a few months after my return from Chicago. In spite of everything, I managed to save myself and return to America, while most of my friends were arrested and some were killed. From that time, my existence was transformed into a life of silent exile—until 1967. Here is how it happened.

In the summer months of 1948, a state of deep depression took hold of me in Chicago because of the events in Palestine. I could do nothing; I didn't want to see anybody. I would go with Carol to the lake shore and sit beside her in silence, not uttering a single word and totally absorbed in worries and dark thoughts. Carol tried from time to time to entertain me, but I warded her off with my silence and black mood, and she would return to her book. I could only frown, my eyes fixed on the distant horizon like a defeated Napoleon in prison on the island of St. Helena.

-27-

By the end of summer, the weather began to change; humidity rose and fog became dense. The trees began to change color. Yellow and red leaves began to fall in the rain. In just three months, I would return to my homeland.

'Abd al-Latif Sukkar arrived from California on his way to Damascus. He was Labib Zuwiyya's friend at the American University of Beirut and his roommate at the British hostel. He had written to me a few days earlier and told me that he was tired of studies and didn't wish to continue, that he had decided to work in commerce with his father in Damascus.

We went for a walk together in the afternoon toward the lake. 'Abd al-Latif told me story after story. Every subject seemed important and enjoyable to him. There were no moments of silence between us, for he did not stop talking. His love adventures in Hollywood amazed me. How true were they? After visiting Paris in the summer of 1946, he had told us for several months about his amorous adventures there. Now I was hearing a rerun, with similar sexual details, but against an American background. I wished 'Abd al-Latif would remain in Chicago. I asked him to. I even insisted, but he had made up his mind to leave on the following day as planned.

The next day, I went with him to the train station. I was sad that he was leaving, but he spoke merrily as usual. Going into his train carriage, he said, "I'll see you in Beirut in three months."

Three months later, we met again in New York, not Beirut. He was living in Great Neck on Long Island, outside New York City. When I stopped by to visit him at the beginning of January 1949 on my way to Beirut, he said he had changed his mind and had decided to work in the field of diplomacy. He had a job at the United Nations Secretariat, a position he had obtained with the help of Faris al-Khuri.

'Abd al-Latif still works at the United Nations. The last time I saw him, however, was in the summer of 1973 in Beirut. He had been transferred to Saudi Arabia to head one of the United Nations offices there. He told me that he had married and divorced twice, that he was married a third time and had two daughters by his third wife. He said he intended to retire shortly and that he had built a home in Brummana, where he would live after he retired. He took me to Ras Beirut in his luxury car, and we promised to see each other again before he left Saudi Arabia and before I returned to Washington. But for some reason we didn't see each other that year, and I never set eyes on him again.

After 'Abd al-Latif had left Chicago, Carol's mother arrived from California. She wanted to live near her daughter. She was a middle-aged woman, rather beautiful. I was depressed at the time and was hardly pleasant to her. I silently carried her bags to the apartment she had rented in the Midway, opposite International House. Then we went to a nearby drugstore to eat. I had no appetite and was overwhelmed by deep melancholy as I drank my coffee. I half listened to the mother and daughter talking to each other, but my mind was distracted, in another world.

A few days later, Muhsin Mahdi arrived, and my morale improved. As soon as he arrived, he rented a room in a house near the university. The next day, I took him to the university and introduced him to Bergstraesser and my other professors. He soon settled down and put his affairs in order. That helped me, for I now had a dear friend close by, someone to share my exile.

-28-

In spite of the presence of Muhsin and Carol, I felt alone with regard to what was happening in my homeland. Carol would sit silently beside me as I read the New York Times, while my Arab friends, including Muhsin, talked about what was happening as if it hardly concerned them.

In June, the first truce was declared. The Zionist Jews established air connections with Czechoslovakia, and weapons and equipment were sent to them in abundance. Then the truce ended, and the Jews attacked on all fronts. The Arabs retreated on all fronts. A second truce was declared in July. By then the Jews had occupied 70 percent of the land of Palestine.

I read in the New York Times one day that the corpses of Iraqi soldiers had been found in a trench near Tulkarm; their hands and feet were tied. They had not been able to escape. I didn't know how true that report was. But I was having a taste of defeat, of humiliation. What would result from the victory of the Jews?

I returned to International House to find some of my Arab friends in the lounge engaged in discussions, their voice rising above all others. Sharp differences arose between the Egyptian and Iraqi students. The argument had turned to words of abuse. Finally, tired, they all went up to their rooms.

I too went up to my room and tried to read but could not. Words danced before my eyes, and I understood nothing of them. I put the book aside and looked for my diary. I jotted down some thoughts, then put it aside. I left my room and walked toward the lake. On the seats in the public park, lovers were whispering to one another and embracing. A cold breeze blew from the lake. I returned to my room, took off my clothes, and fell into bed, overcome finally by exhaustion.

-29-

Fall arrived quickly, and the climate changed all of a sudden. The sky was clear and of a very deep blue color. It was filled with big, white clouds. The waves of the lake rose higher. Their spray began to reach the Outer Drive, making it slippery for cars. Trees turned a golden yellow. Chicago reminded me of winter in Beirut. I walked daily along the lakeshore, now empty of people. I would sit on a nearby bench and let the mist wet my face. I imagined I was at the Corniche in Beirut on a stormy day.

The moment of return was approaching day by day. I would be home in less than three months. The images of people and places that I had suppressed deep inside me were returning to consciousness: faces of friends and comrades, the face of Sa'adah, the streets of Ras Beirut, the cafés of the Rocher, Faysal's Restaurant.

I gave free reign to my dreams for the first time since my arrival in Chicago. I missed hearing my own language, spoken by my people, my beloved ones, my countrymen. Suddenly, everything changed around me. I began to look around me with the eyes of a traveler ready to depart.

I received my grades for the summer term: they were excellent. My director asked me to specify the topic of my thesis. I thought about it for a few days, then presented him with a topic he accepted directly: "The Problem of Values in the Philosophy of Nicolai Hartmann and C. I. Lewis."

Hartmann was an idealist in his style, despite the fact that he was a follower of Husserl, and his ideas exerted great influence on contemporary existentialist philosophy (specifically on Heidegger, Sartre, and Merleau-Ponty). Hartmann considered such moral values as justice, courage, love, and friendship to be objective and timeless. For him, those values enjoyed an eternal existence, like Plato's Ideas. His style was extremely precise, elegant, and beautiful. Perhaps this was what attracted me to him most, besides the fact that he had written his book during the First World War as a soldier fighting in the trenches.

Hartmann represented the European philosophical tradition in the deepest sense; C. I. Lewis, the strongest expression of Anglo-American pragmatism. The difference between them was clearest in the problem of values. In Lewis's view, values are relative and determined by individual experience; what is good or desirable has no meaning outside direct experience. Although Lewis tried to preserve the objective quality of values and insisted that they are not mere personal judgments, he succeeded in taking them away from the philosophical background, on which in Hartmann's view they depended, and subjected them to an empirical logic that did not accept postulates of ideas outside direct sensory experience.

I don't know exactly why I chose this subject. Perhaps because I wanted to argue that Hartmann was right and that values were absolute and not relative. In spite of the influence on me of Sa'adah and of his philosophy steeped in German historical theory, I hadn't shaken the idealist philosophies of my early education, strengthened as these had been by my studies at the American University of Beirut. I rejected Lewis's philosophy in advance and accepted Hartmann's. I wanted to use the one to refute the other. What did I expect to achieve in the process? I don't know.

I had to finish my thesis before November 1, to be able to graduate at the end of 1948. I confined myself to my room for the duration of four weeks, from the middle of September to the middle of October, having borrowed from the library all the books and sources I needed, in addition to a complete set of *Ethics*, a journal that was (and still is) published by the philosophy department at the University of Chicago. My day began at half past seven in the morning. I went over the notes I had taken the previous night on my readings in *Ethics* and other sources. I wrote from nine o'clock until one, when hunger would oblige me to stop. I went downstairs to the cafeteria and ate lunch by myself, most of the other students having eaten by then. After lunch, I returned to my room, read and took notes for two hours, then resumed writing until five o'clock. At five, I went out to the Midway for a walk until suppertime at six. I ate a light supper, then went upstairs to my room to continue reading and taking notes until midnight.

Writing these lines now, I try to recall the experience of working on my thesis. In front of me is a copy of the thesis, which I have kept all these years. I scan a few pages of it now, and I am amazed at its idiomatic language and strong structure. Are these ideas and analyses actually my own, or did I derive them from the books and articles I had read and the notes I had taken from them?

What are the dividing lines between scholarship, plagiarism, and simple theft?

My thesis was accepted without impediment, and a time was set for the oral defense. It was to take place on an afternoon in December in the office of the chairman of the philosophy department. Three other classmates of mine had submitted their theses, and their oral examinations were scheduled for the same afternoon. We all sat waiting in the hall outside. We had our best suits on. My necktie felt tight around my neck, and sweat trickled down my forehead. The waiting room, like the rest of the building, was overheated. The chairman called in one of my friends. He entered the room, and the door was closed behind him. We waited in silence. Half an hour later, he came out, a pale smile on his face. We asked him how it had gone.

"There are four," he said, "and one of them is Rudolf Carnap!"

Rudolf Carnap was a member of the philosophy faculty and the most famous professor of philosophy in the United States. He was of Austrian origin and a colleague of Fitzenstein, one of the pillars of logical positivism. He had taken refuge in the United States after the Nazis occupied Austria, and had taught at several American universities before finally settling down at the University of Chicago. This piece of information worried us. I was third in line. The minutes passed heavily before the second candidate ended his examination and came out wiping the sweat from his brow. Then the chairman called me. I stepped into the room, my heart pounding. I sat on a chair facing the four professors. The first one I set my eyes on was Carnap. I knew who he was because I had seen him in the corridor of Swift Hall, but I had never taken any of his courses. He was about 50 years old and wore glasses. He smiled at me, but that did not allay my fear. The chairman of the committee opened the floor for questions. I don't remember now any of the specific questions, only that they dealt with my methodology and with some problems related to the premises on which my research and analysis depended. When Carnap's turn came, he addressed me in a quiet tone and with extreme kindness. I knew that his philosophical position completely contradicted the one I had adopted, which was that of Hartmann. But he did not raise this issue at all and limited his questions to matters of detail and theoretical definitions. He nodded his head positively at my answers, which helped me to regain some of my courage and to elaborate. The examination ended amazingly quickly. I went out, my head teeming with ideas, thinking of the answers I could and should have given but hadn't, and I wished, to no avail, for another opportunity to answer the questions I'd been asked.

The graduation ceremony was held in Rockefeller Chapel on December 19, and I was handed my diploma by Robert Hutchner, president of the university. It was the last graduation ceremony that Hutchner presided over, for he had submitted his resignation, after having spent about 20 years as president. He had been only 30 years old when he was appointed. Going up onto the platform, Hutchner looked young despite his stout stature. He gave a short speech. The ceremony ended within half an hour.

After the ceremony, the chapel yard was crowded with students and their relatives who exchanged congratulations, talked with one another, and laughed. I stood to the side of the crowd with Carol, who had been waiting for me at the entrance. In her hand was a large package tied with a colored ribbon. She kissed me on both cheeks and said, "On the occasion of your graduation."

Her gift to me was Bulfinch's book of Greek mythology in an especially elegant edition that pleased me very much. I lost this book along with the many others that stayed at International House when I left Chicago. My books were later divided up among my friends there, and I don't know whose good fortune it was to take the book that Carol had given me on my graduation in 1948.

-30-

Christmas was over, and I was to leave in a few days. I had many things to do before leaving Chicago.

How strange was the feeling that came over me those last few days. As the date of my departure drew near, I began to feel the agony of separation. Carol and I revisited the places where we had spent many long summer hours, which now appeared to have been happy ones. We went to Stony Island Park, which was empty. Its high trees were bare; leaves littered the ground that used to be covered with flowers and green grass. The lake was frozen, and the cold wind whistled over it. Rain began to fall on us suddenly as we were walking on the desolate shore, so we returned to International House.

I borrowed $400 from Muhsin, of which I used $300 to buy a third-class ticket for passage on board an Italian ship from New York to Genoa, and I paid $20 for the train ticket from Chicago to New York. I had $80 left, and my plan was to stop in Switzerland for a week to visit Usama (who had been transferred to the Iraqi consulate there the previous year), and then I would somehow manage the rest of my trip from Genoa to Beirut.

On the day of my departure, I awoke early. I looked around my room and remembered the day I had arrived in Chicago and the promise I hade made to return home within a year. I had kept my promise, but I had no feelings of victory. Pain, like desire, changes with time and becomes less sharp. I carried my luggage and went downstairs to the lounge. Nobody but Carol was there. She was sitting on a large sofa in a far corner of the lounge and didn't see me at first. She was wearing the fur coat and hat that she had worn the first evening we spent together at the High Hat. She looked small and lost, sitting on that large sofa. She had become lonely even before I had gone. When she became aware of my presence, she turned toward me and smiled. I carried my luggage to the taxi that waited for us at the door. She insisted on accompanying me to the station. In the taxi, she said, as she put her hand in mine, "Don't forget to send me a letter as soon as you reach Bern."

"I'll write you a letter every day on board the ship, and I'll mail the letters, all at one time, on my arrival in Genoa."

We did not speak much in the taxi.

The railway station was crowded. A porter took my luggage, and Carol and I walked behind him. We reached the train, and the porter put my luggage in the place reserved for me in advance. Carol and I embraced silently; then I got on the train and stood at the window and looked at her. When the train began moving, she said something I did not hear from behind the glass of the window.

I waved to her. I saw her take a handkerchief from her handbag and wipe her eyes. The tears she had suppressed at the moment of separation were flowing now. She was still waving her handkerchief as she gradually disappeared from my sight forever.

In New York, 'Abd al-Latif was waiting for me at Grand Central Station when I arrived the next morning. We carried my suitcases to the ship company, then went to the United Nations, where he introduced me to his colleagues and showed me his office over-looking the river. He was proud of his position and wanted to prove to me the extent of his success. When one of the secretaries entered he talked to her in his particular way in order to give me the subtle impression that he had a special relationship with her.

In the afternoon, he took me for a drive in his new car to Great Neck on Long Island, which is about three quarters of an hour from New York City, where he lived in a large apartment. We sat somewhere and talked until supper time, then we drove back to a restaurant near his home and had our supper. After that, we went to a nearby cinema, where we saw a boring American movie. When I went to bed, it was almost midnight.

We woke up early the next day. I needed to board the ship before nine in the morning. We had breakfast quickly and rushed to the car, even 'Abd al-Latif drinking his coffee from a cup he took with him to the car. The sky was cloudy; rain threatened. When we entered the port at Pier 42, the passengers had begun to board the beautiful Italian ship, which appeared big and luxurious. Its name was written in large letters on its bow: *Vulcania*. 'Abd al-Latif stopped at the bottom of the steps and gave me a warm farewell. I climbed up the stairs and stood at the railing of the deck, waving at him. He walked to his car and drove away, and I went to look for the place reserved for me. I met one of the ship's officers and showed him my ticket. He said, "This is a third-class ticket, and you're in first class now. You have to go down to the bottom of the stairs, then left to the stern of the ship."

I descended the stairs and walked through what resembled a subterranean passage until I reached a closed door. I opened it and found myself in a large hall with bunk beds that could accommo-date more than 100 people. The hall was crowded with people, mostly Italians. I stood there for a moment, not knowing what to do. How could I live in this hall for eleven days? Most of the beds had been taken, but, after some effort, I found an empty top bunk. I put my luggage on it and stood to look around me. I was over-taken by deep consternation. Suddenly, I thought there must be a place that looked over the sea, where I could sit during the day at least. When I tried to go out the door through which I had entered, an officer stopped me, saying, "Where are you going?"

"I need some fresh air. I'm about to suffocate."

"It's forbidden for third-class passengers to leave this place. If you want to breathe some fresh air, you have to go to the stern of this ship, this way."

And he pointed to the place.

It was an open space at the stern, not very much higher than sea level. The floor was piled with rope. In one corner, I saw a chair of the sort used on beaches. I took it to the Italian waiter who supervised the dining hall and told him that I wanted to reserve it for myself for the duration of the trip; I gave him a few dollars. It worked, and I spent most of the days of the voyage on this chair, leaving it only at mealtimes and at sunset. I read, thought, and observed the sea rise and fall around me. I had two books with me: one of them was *Oliver Twist* by Charles Dickens, and the other was Thomas Mann's *The Magic Mountain*. I put Dickens' book aside and began reading *The Magic Mountain*, which consisted of several hundred pages in small print. The hero of the novel, Hans Castorp, a young man from the middle class, is stricken by tuberculosis and is advised by the doctor to go to a sanitarium on the top of a mountain in the Swiss Alps. There, in the magical world surrounding the sanitarium, Hans gets acquainted with a number of the sanitarium's residents, whose ideas, tastes, and patterns of life represent European bourgeois society as it was before the First World War. Hans engages them in long conversations that form the bulk of the book and represent the essence of European civilization as well as the political and religious ideas prevalent at that time. The novel ends soon after the outbreak of the First World War, as Hans, who has joined the German army, dies in its first days.

When I was tired of reading, I wrapped myself with a wool blanket that the waiter had managed to provide me with, and I closed my eyes and tried to sleep for a few minutes. Most of the passengers remained within the hold of the ship because of the increasing cold and the rain. Before we reached the Strait of Gibraltar, a severe storm arose, and most of the passengers, seasick, stayed in bed. The restaurant was empty except for two or three passengers who sat at my table. We ate while holding our plates, lest they should slide off to the floor. In spite of the storm, I continued to sit outdoors, where I had found a place sheltered from the rain near the door of the hold. In those conditions, I could not read. Spray would wet the pages of the book if I opened it, so I put it away. Sometimes the wind was so strong that I could not hold the pages of the book down. While the winds blew around me, I sat thus, motionless for hours on end. Whenever I remember those hours, I feel slightly ashamed of myself. I think I passed through something like a religious experience.... I regressed to adolescence, to that age in which one experiences the most difficult moments of one's emotional and intellectual life. At that age, I had done nothing without first reciting the Opening Sura of the Qur'an (Qur'an 1) three times and "Say: God, He is One" (Qur'an 112) at least once—and that in a compulsive manner. I used to do that before every class, before going to sleep, before taking the tramway, and before swimming. With the winds blowing around me, I also returned to pre-adolescence, to childhood, and to the images and imaginings of childhood that had protected me and given me reassurance and tranquility. In the midst of the worst weather, huddled on deck, my thoughts were absorbed in religious subjects fastened on the Prophet Muhammad, who appeared to me then as a saving and guiding hero; thus consoled, I let my soul anchor itself for a while in a distant, familiar, and beloved world....

The grip of that whole experience, a passing psychological state, lifted as soon as we reached Gibraltar. But the experience revealed to me an aspect of myself whose existence I had not suspected. I realized that the tendency to return to the past, for individuals as well as groups, was a tendency deeply rooted in the self, one that appears in conditions of danger and in circumstances of loneliness and anxiety, and I realized that one should guard oneself against it.

In our routine, daily life, we seldom realize that there are points of weakness and fear nestled deep in our souls. At the moment when our life leaves its regular pattern, such as in cases of travel to far-off places, or in conditions of sickness or imprisonment, our internal defenses collapse, and we fall prey to fear and anxiety. In those circumstances, we often revert to childhood and to the religious beliefs and superstitions we learned at an early age, or we yearn for mother's lap and father's protection, and for those who represent them in our lives. And to the extent that fear and anxiety are basic motives for returning to the past, to that extent will such return be neurotic, closer to sickness than to health, because it represents an escape from a present situation and a refusal to face reality. A long time passed before I understood my strange experience on board the *Vulcania* and comprehended its truth. And to this day, I don't know what has enabled me to resist the attraction of the past, to refuse the illusions of childhood, and to go forth on the path of objective rationality.

—*Four*—

-1-

It was half past five in the morning when the ship anchored in the port of Beirut. The sun had not yet risen from behind Mount Sinnin, but the gray of dawn was beginning to change into a pink light that scattered the fog stretching all along the shore from the Bay of Junieh to the Beirut River. Soon it filled the sky with silvery and golden colors.

I scanned those standing on the pier near the stairs that were lowered from the ship, but I didn't see any of my friends. I had expected that Joseph or Raja or Fu'ad or all of them would be there to receive me. I was disappointed. Then suddenly, I heard a voice calling me and saw a man I didn't know coming toward me. He said that Raja sent him and that he worked in Raja's office as a customs broker. He asked about my luggage, and I pointed to my only suitcase, next to me. We left the customs house within minutes and took a taxi to Ras Beirut.

The Beirut streets were empty at that hour. On Weygand Street a man was opening his shop, and on Bab Idris Street the only shop open was a confectioner's. The Frères' school beyond the Sa'atiyya Reservoir was closed. We passed Graham Station… the American University's Hospital… Bliss Avenue… Faysal's Restaurant.

I asked the taxi driver to go to Jeanne D'Arc Street. Joseph, I knew, lived there in Fakhri's mother's house. I knocked on the door loudly. When I entered, the house came alive, laughter rang out, and conversation flowed with questions, stories, and jokes. Joseph said that no one had come to receive me because my arrival had been expected a day earlier. In fact, everyone had gone to the port to receive me at six in the morning on the previous day, but when my ship had not arrived and since the company representative had announced that he did not know its exact time of arrival, Raja had asked his employee to monitor the arrival on the next day of ships sailing from Italy. Thus had he received me on arriving. I took my first breakfast in Beirut with Joseph, his brother George, and Fawzi al-Ma'luf. It consisted of oil and thyme, white cheese, olives, and carob molasses with tahini. After breakfast, Joseph took me in his old Ford to where my mother lived with my grandfather's family.

She met me with tears flowing from her eyes. My brother Khalid had died only two days earlier. He had suffered a lot and was only eighteen years old. I had brought a gift for him. It was in my pocket: a round pocket watch. He had liked watches of all kinds and had owned many. Had he lived longer, he might have become a watch repairman. I have never known anyone else who wanted to pursue that profession.

I kissed my grandmother's hand, as I had since childhood, and I embraced my paternal aunt and my two maternal aunts. When I asked about my grandfather, my grandmother said his health was not as good as one wished. He was sitting in a dark corner of the room, watching but estranged from what was happening. I'm not sure that he recognized me. He had changed a lot in one year. His hair was white and had not been touched by scissors for a long time. His robe was old and torn, and yet this was the man who had always worn the most elegant clothes and had taken great care of his appearance. I shook hands with Khayriyya Hanim, and she kissed me and wept. Her home—comprising two rooms, a kitchen, and a bathroom—was exactly as I remembered it from my visits as a student in preparatory school. On feast days, she used to give me two liras, a sum that used to make me feel extravagantly rich for two weeks.

In the afternoon, I went to visit the Leader (Sa'adah's house was not very far from Khayriyya Hanim's). Sa'adah was expecting me. I saluted him in the Party manner. How often had I dreamt in Chicago of this moment! He embraced me and asked me about myself, my arrival, my trip. We entered his office and sat together for some two hours, during which time he honored me with a survey of the condition of the Party, a political analysis of the country, and his thought on the Palestine question, which had taken hold of all of his attention. He said, "The present leaders are all bankrupt. They were the ones who led us to this catastrophe. How can salvation be at their hands?"

The Party was the only hope, in his view. Conditions must be changed so that the Party could come to power and take control.

"Armed conflict is the only way to free Palestine."

This was what he believed to the end.

As he was saying goodbye to me, he added, "I want you to be here tomorrow morning. There are many things waiting for you to do."

-2-

I woke up early the next day in the room that my mother had rented for me in a Syrian woman's home, situated in the middle of the slope leading to the Military Beach, near where the Manara Pharmacy stands today. I took a bath, dressed, and walked out onto Bliss Avenue. When I reached the Hubaysh police station, I saw the tramway slowing down at the stop nearby. I ran to catch it, but it had not stopped for long and was now moving again, so I grasped its back door and leaped onto its rear steps, holding on until we reached Jubran's shop. I jumped off the tram before it stopped, in the clever way we had learned so well during our undergraduate days. Jubran had opened his barber shop at dawn, as has been his custom to this day. I greeted him and we talked a little, then I continued on my way to Fakhri's mother's home, where I had breakfast with Joseph, George, and Fawzi.

At about eight o'clock, the streets of Ras Beirut were alive with movement. Joseph took me in his car to the Leader's home, and we parted on the understanding that we would meet at noon at Faysal's.

The Leader's home was crowded with people. A delegation of Party members had arrived that morning from Damascus. I sat in the sitting room waiting for the Leader. From a distance, I saw a short man with short hair. It was George 'Abd al-Masih. He was speaking with those around him in his low, deep voice. I walked over to him. When he saw me, a wide smile spread over his face, and he embraced me warmly. We exchanged a few words. (In all the time I knew him, our exchanges were invariably short: a few words sufficed for us to understand each other perfectly.) Then he went out to ascertain that the Leader's car was ready.

After about half an hour, the Leader finished his meeting with the Syrian (a Damascene) delegation, and he came out of his office and gestured to me to follow him. We took the car waiting for us to the office of *Al-Jil al-Jadid* (The new generation) at Khan Anton Bey. George 'Abd al-Masih sat beside the driver, and I sat in the backseat, to the Leader's left. The Leader always liked to sit in the backseat on the right side.

Khan Anton Bey was an old building and one of the most beautiful historical buildings in Beirut. It was at the end of the slope of

Bab Idris Street and was open to the sea on the north and west sides. The Khan had been built in the middle of the nineteenth century in the old Ottoman style. In the middle of it was a large courtyard surrounded on the ground level by shops, commercial firms, cafés, and a restaurant; in the upper stories, there were apartments and suites used for various purposes. The offices of *Al-Jil al-Jadid* and its press, the printing press also of *Al-Shams* (The Sun), were in one of the suites on the third floor. The old press stood in the middle of the hall and the surrounding rooms were used as editorial offices. The one on the extreme right was the editor-in-chief's office, which the Leader used when he visited the newspaper's premises. When the machines started printing the newspaper at around noon, they shook the floor rhythmically and their sound was deafening. I was sometimes afraid that the floor would cave in and we would all fall through—with the press and the desks—and land on top of those living on the second and ground floors. I pleaded constantly with the Leader to move the newspaper to another press. He eventually agreed. And that was the beginning of a chain of events leading to the disaster.

-3-

The Party had little income at that time other than its membership fees and the gifts it received from émigré comrades. The Leader's family income was limited to what his wife received regularly from her relatives in Argentina. The amount was not sufficient to cover the family's expenses and hospitality. The Party's financial committee was unable to solve the problem, and it was getting worse every day. The solution came unexpectedly, thanks to the intelligence of Fayiza Antippa, one of the earliest Party comrades and Fakhri Ma'luf's sister. She organized a series of tea parties every Sunday at the Beirut home of one of the Syrian Social Nationalists. The teas were attended by the Leader. Nationalist guests and their friends contributed one lira each. In the winter and spring of 1949, these tea parties evolved into large Party meetings and were attended by thousands of Nationalists and Party supporters. To them, the Leader delivered many of his speeches that, as a collection, constitute the core of his writings from this last period of his life.

I attended every single one of the parties with the Leader. I particularly remember going to one of them, perhaps because it was held at the beginning of spring or because it was held a short while before the disaster happened. It was to be held at the home of one of the comrades, at Shuwayfat. We took the car at about four o'clock and drove along the Rocher road toward al-Ramla al-Bayda'. The leader sat silently, looking out to his right at the sea, which was calm after the winter storms and as green as the spring grass. Suddenly, he began singing an aria in Italian from one of Verdi's operas. I looked at him in astonishment, and he turned toward me smiling as he continued to sing as loud as he could. Anyone hearing him would have thought he hadn't a single worry in the world. In fact, I never once saw him surrender to worry or anxiety. Matters of the moment used to occupy his full attention, and he put aside all other considerations. I know no other person who lived in the present, moment by moment and hour by hour, as Sa'adah did. The possibility of death did not concern him, and life as such did not mean much to him.

A large crowd was always waiting for us outside whatever house the party took place in. The Nationalists arranged guards of honor to give the Leader the Party salute. I walked a few steps behind the Leader and saw the Nationalists look at him as he surveyed them and raised his hand in salute. I saw dignity and pride in their looks. When he stood up to deliver a speech to them, he saw fighting heroes before him, the only ones who would save the nation. They derived enormous self-confidence from him, and he drew his own confidence in the Party from them.

-4-

One day Sa'adah called me into his office at home. I found him sitting and reading *Al-Jil al-Jadid*. When he saw me, he put the newspaper down on the desk and said, pointing to an article on the third page, "Have you read this article?"

It was an article by George 'Atiyyah on 'Abd al-Rahman al-Kawakibi.

"Yes, I've read it."

"Have you any remarks on it?"

No, I did not have any remarks on the subject. It was clear that something in the article occupied the Leader's mind. What was it? At that moment, we heard a knock on the door and Labib Zuwiyya entered. He had begun working for the cultural committee a few hours per day. Sa'adah asked him whether he had read the article.

"A good article, Mr. Leader."

Signs of displeasure appeared on the Leader's face. He began to read the article aloud and reached the sentence where George had said that he (i.e., George) had discovered 'Abd al-Rahman al-Kawakibi. The Leader paused and said, "George 'Atiyyah, then, is the one who discovered this Syrian philosopher, and he is the first to write on him!"

Suddenly I realized what he meant. It was not George 'Atiyyah but rather he himself who had uncovered the importance of al-Kawakibi: it was he (the Leader) who had been the first to write on him. In fact, Sa'adah had mentioned al-Kawakibi in a number of his articles, and George should have referred to this. The lack of a reference was the cause of this tiresome scene. The Leader wanted to remind us that Sa'adah was the source of everything to do with the Party: its Leader, its theoretician, its legislator, and the sole reviver of the nation; nobody else was to rival him in this regard, nobody else could.

-5-

Days passed quickly and I settled down into a daily routine revolving around intellectual and cultural matters in the life of the Party. At the beginning of spring, I began to write an article a week for *Al-Jil al-Jadid* under the general title "Our New Life," and signed "Zaynon" (Xenophon). I gave the first article to Wadi' al-Ashqar, the editor in chief. He published it without comment on the fourth page. The second and third articles appeared in the same place. But I was surprised to see the fourth article on the first page, in the column reserved for the Leader's editorials. This was by order of the Leader, I later learned. Thus, "Our New Life" continued to appear in this prominent fashion to the end, when the last issue of *Al-Jil al-Jadid* was burned along with the offices of the newspaper on June 10, 1949. In the meantime, the Leader issued a decree appointing me deputy chairman for culture and editor in chief of the Party's monthly magazine, *Al-Nizam al-Jadid* (The new order).

Instead of going to the Leader's house every day, I began to go directly to the newspaper office at Khan Anton Bey. I sat with Wadi' or George in the room overlooking the port, and we discussed matters related to the newspaper and the magazine. I spent most of the morning at the newspaper office. Occasionally, the Leader called the press to ask about me or to arrange a visit, and so I would stay there until he arrived. He often forgot all about lunchtime when he was preoccupied, so when that happened I would not eat before three or four o'clock. On these occasions, we used to ask for broiled meat and chickpea dip to be delivered by the restaurant, and we ate standing up around one of the desks as the ground shook under us with the movement of the presses.

On the days on which the Leader was otherwise occupied, I went to the press that printed *Al-Nizam al-Jadid,* situated on one of the narrow streets off al-Dabbas Square. I sometimes took the tramway from Bab Idris to Martyrs' Square (al-Burj), and sometimes went on foot by way of al-Ma'rad Street and the Grand Theater, then behind the La'azariyya to al-Dabbas Square. Before my return to Beirut, *Al-Nizam al-Jadid* was printed at the newspaper press, without any special effort in its layout or artistic production. I decided on a new design, with a color cover and new fonts. I made an agreement with a small printing press owned by a young Nationalist from Dik al-Mahdi who was a relative of Asad al-Ashqar. *Al-Nizam al-Jadid* appeared in its new design at the beginning of June and caused a big fury inside and outside the Party.

The first issue began with the Leader's fifth lecture, delivered at the cultural symposium that had been revived in 1948. In it he explained in detail the Party's principles and its social and political aims (these lectures were published in Damascus in 1950 under the title *The Ten Lectures at the Cultural Symposium in 1948* and were reprinted many times). It is worth mentioning that the fifth lecture was the last that the Leader had an opportunity to revise prior to publication. The remaining five lectures were sent unrevised to the press, as taken down in writing by George 'Abd al-Masih.

In addition to the note by the editor in chief, I wrote an article entitled "The Philosophy of Values in the Materio-Spiritual School" over the signature "Deputy Chairman for Cultural and Fine Arts."

In the editorial, I dealt with the role of the Party in the crisis that the country was passing through. I said:

> When the Palestine crisis broke out at the beginning of 1948, the executive general of Haifa asked strongly that the Party save the Southern cause by direct intervention in the military actions that had begun to take place at the time. The Leader's answer to the executive general of Haifa was that the [Syrian] Social Nationalists form the second—and last—rows of defense. The inevitable fall of the first rows will make the Social Nationalists the nation's only hope.
>
> Now that the first haphazard rows have fallen as the Leader had prophesied, the Nationalist movement has become the nation's only hope.

I ended it with:

> The Syrians of yesteryear, Syrians of failure and humiliation and defeat, are now dying; and in their midst arise the Syrians of tomorrow, Syrians of dignity and glory and victory.
>
> The Social Nationalists are the heroes of the Age of the Renaissance (al-Nahda) and the creators of Syrian idealism.

In the article I discussed materio-spiritual philosophy. That was the beginning of my specialization in this school, and I later became the only Party expert who could unlock the mysteries of this new philosophy. After rebuilding the Party in Damascus in 1950, George 'Abd al-Masih used to say to those who asked him about materio-spiritual philosophy, as did Hanna Dumyan one day, "Wait until Hisham returns from America, for he will explain it to you."

In this new issue of *Al-Nizam al-Jadid*, In'am Ra'd wrote an article entitled "Settlement Parties in the Balance," George 'Atiyya wrote an analysis of the epic of Gilgamesh, and Faruq Nassar wrote a poem entitled "Gift of Time." There were also three unsigned book reviews, two of which were on *Tariq al-Khalas* (The road to salvation) by Dr. George Hanna and the third was on *Ma'na al-Nakba* (The meaning of the catastrophe) by Dr. Qustantin Zurayq—and I think they were all written by the Leader.

-6-

A few days before the appearance of *Al-Nizam al-Jadid*, a meeting was held at Hani Baltaji's home in Ras Beirut. The Leader gave a speech there and announced that the Party had run out of patience and that confrontation with the ruling clique was inevitable. This speech had a direct influence on the authorities' decision to deal the Party a lethal blow.

We arrived at Hani's home at about six o'clock. The weather was stormy: it rained heavily then stopped, but the wind continued to blow violently. The hall and the surrounding rooms were crowded with Nationalists, and so was the little garden surrounding the house. A few minutes before the Leader spoke, George 'Abd al-Masih entered the hall and whispered in the Leader's ear in an audible voice, overheard by all around, that government security forces had taken positions in the street in front of the house, that they were preventing the Social Nationalists from entering the premises, and that the officer responsible had asked that the meeting be immediately disbanded or else he would be obliged to use force to break it up.

This information spread with lightning speed through the hall and the surrounding rooms and into the garden. Silence reigned, and only the sound of the police outside and the wind blowing in the surrounding trees could be heard. I saw Sa'adah's face turn red with rage, but he quickly contained himself and smiled as he always did when suppressing a strong emotion. He asked George 'Abd al-Masih to try to cool down the Social Nationalists and prevent them from provoking the police for any reason whatsoever. It was clear that the aim of the authorities was to create an incident that would justify disbanding the meeting.

I was sitting next to two brothers who were Party comrades. The younger had a revolver, which he took out of his pocket. The older brother wanted the revolver in order to join the Leader's bodyguard outside, but the younger brother opposed him because he wanted it for himself. The revolver changed hands, and the discussion became heated. I was afraid that the weapon would go off and that a bullet would hit one of those present, so I suggested that both should join the bodyguard and use the revolver jointly if shooting started. They both looked at me strangely for a moment, then rushed outside without a word.

Tension in the hall was rising. From the window, I saw the Leader's bodyguard build their barricades in the garden. I saw a revolver and Tommy guns like those carried by the Social Nationalists in the mountains when the Leader was being pursued. I thought, "This time, it's going to be a real fight," and I was overwhelmed by fear. My heart was pounding.

Suddenly silence reigned in the hall and spread like a calm breeze to the neighboring room, the garden, and the street. I turned around and saw the Leader standing on a table in the middle of the hall and looking, motionless, at those present. He remained thus for a few moments. In the encompassing silence, attentive eyes... held breaths... throbbing hearts.

He uttered his first words in a calm, serious voice as though he were speaking in a classroom, and his strong voice filled the stillness all around. The tension disappeared and was replaced by confidence and reassurance. I noticed the change on the faces of the Social Nationalists, in their looks, and in the way they stood.

"We grew up looking for a fight," he began. "The fight never looked for us. We grew up with a dignity that defined our existence, and we will not give up the meaning of our existence for anything in the world.... We are the soldiers of a renaissance that fights on all fronts because its war is a war for this nation, a war for the nation's victory over foreign and domestic interests bent on humiliating a nation that refuses humiliation.

"We fought and continue to fight internal enslavement that takes the shape of feudalism, capitalism, and greed for self-interests and benefits to the individual. Had it not been for this internal enslavement allied with an external enslavement, we would not have lost Cilicia nor Alexandretta nor Palestine.

"... The kettle of renaissance is boiling, this renaissance is roaring, and woe to anyone who tries to stand in its way."

He said the last sentence with power and vehemence, and in a clearly threatening tone of voice. The hall shook with applause, and I saw him raise his hand to require silence. His rage had changed into a cool fire burning in his eyes. He said in a voice that rent the silence, "The most bitter war is an internal war, a war waged against us by those who should be called upon by national honor to fight on our side, not opposite us.

"The era of the herd is over and that of the living, rational group has begun.

"We have not committed aggression against anyone, we have not attacked anyone. If attacked, we will not be sheep, but lions."[13]

The Social Nationalists broke out again in loud acclaim. When the meeting ended, the Leader left, surrounded by his bodyguard, and I walked behind him. Out in the street, the policemen who had frightened us stood pinned to their positions. The Leader walked in front of them slowly and ceremoniously as though they were magnificent honor guards come to greet him.

-7-

A few days later, we celebrated the First of March, 1949: the Leader was 45 years old. Who could have known it would be the last celebration? The future extended endlessly before us, we thought....

Who were the Party's enemies? Who were those who wanted to put an end to it?

What do these names mean today: Riyad al-Sulh, Bishara al-Khuri, Husni al-Za'im, Muhsin al-Barazi?

But they succeeded.

The sectarian, the feudal, and the reactionary forces in constant conflict with one another were able to conspire against the Party and stop Antun Sa'adah.

How did these forces succeed?

When I recall what the Leader used to say in his speeches about the Party's size and power, I realize how wrong he was in his assessment of the Party, of its real power. Perhaps he exaggerated its size purposely. On the First of March, 1943, for example, he spoke in a celebration in Argentina of "tens and hundreds of thousands of Syrians who adopted the Social Nationalist faith," assuring his listeners in the city of Cordoba that they were part of a large whole that had great strength: "You meet here to join your will to that of hundreds of thousands of Social Nationalists, who, I feel and know, are with us in this meeting as we are with them in theirs."[14]

He used to speak of the Party as if it were an actual government on the verge of taking power. In his personal behavior and public stance, he acted like a man of state. The Party in his view was the only political force that stood up to colonialism and could achieve independence. It was the only force that could liberate Palestine. I think that Sa'adah underestimated the depth of sectarian, tribal, and feudal feelings in the country. He was genuinely perplexed at the masses' hesitancy to support the Party. Despite the sympathy that the Party met with in certain circles, the number of its members did not reach "tens and hundreds of thousands," as Sa'adah claimed. After the surge in popular interest that followed Sa'adah's return to Beirut in 1947, the Party's growth was slow and limited to certain areas and classes. Its greatest failure was its inability to attract the poorer working and agricultural classes. The proportion of workers and peasants in its membership was low while the petite bourgeoisie dominated its cadres and leadership in the directorships, the executive committees, and the regional centers.

At the time, I didn't realize all of this. I wanted what the other members of the rising generation to which I belonged wanted—namely, a radical transformation of our corrupt society. What we wanted was revolution. But revolution for us was something theoretical, a romantic event: we would seize power and change the direction of history. There was no clear role for the masses in our theories. The Party was elitist in its structure, in its discipline, in its members' relationships. It utterly lacked a class perspective because the idea of the nation, not of a revolutionary class, was its pivotal doctrine. We rejected the concept of class because it contradicted the nationalist concept and negated the theory of the nation. Thus, the idol of the nation concealed the reality of the masses from our vision, and idealist thinking separated us from social reality. The Party remained a limited movement with regard to size and numbers, and it was unable to mobilize the masses and to enter the political battle imposed on us after the Leader's return. Because it was out of touch, the Party was unable to realize the victory that Sa 'adah thought was just within our reach.

-8-

Outside work hours, I used to spend most of my free time at the Leader's home. I don't know how I managed my life from day to day. I was not shouldering my responsibility toward my family, which had forfeited all it owned. I lost all personal ambition, and the Party took possession of all my activities.

The Leader would sometimes invite me on weekends to walk with him along the Corniche. We used to walk, back and forth, from 'Ayn al-Mraysah to the Military Beach, unaware of the passage of time. We were accompanied by his private guard 'Ali, a Palestinian from 'Akka who had joined the Party while still a sergeant in the British police force. I can see him before me now in an old military overcoat that reached down to his ankles, raising his arm and greeting the Leader each time we turned around during our walk along the Corniche. On Sunday, we sometimes went before noon to the Chalet Suisse at the Dawrah or the Ghaylani café at the Rocher. The Leader did not mind if one of my friends accompanied us—Joseph Salamah or Labib Zuwiyya and, of course, Fu'ad Najjar. We spent the afternoon hours talking and drinking coffee or tea. In those days, orange groves extended all the way from Antilyas to the Dawra and Sinn al-Fil. The fragrance of orange blossoms filled the air and the car whenever we went to the Chalet Suisse, and it reminded me of my childhood in Jaffa. Today, it reminds me of the Leader in the last springtime of his life.

Let us return to that last celebration of the First of March. We wanted to hold it at the Normandy Hotel, but the authorities forbade us, so we held it at the home of Fu'ad and Iskandar Shawi. The rain was pouring heavily that night. The invitations sent to many personages outside the Party were annulled, a number of other invited persons did not show up because of the change of time and place, and so the size of the gathering was much smaller than we had expected.

In spite of these contretemps, the hall was crowded. The Leader sat in the place of honor in the hall and, contrary to his usual demeanor at such occasions, he was uncharacteristically silent and lost in deep thought. I had never known him to be so silent. But I didn't give the matter much thought because I had prepared a speech, which I had to deliver in just a few minutes. I was preceded by several speakers, the last of whom was 'Abd Allah Qubrusi. When my turn came, I stood in front of the Leader. He smiled encouragingly. My speech was full of grammatical errors. I said many things that I don't remember now. All that remains in my memory is the silence that suddenly reigned when the master of ceremonies called out my name to deliver my speech, the sound of rain falling on the closed windows, the Leader's face in a spot of dim light surrounded by the faces of dear comrades, of which many have disappeared since that ill-fated year. I don't know to this day what happened to many of the others. Sa'adah looked at me attentively, listening to every word I said. He clapped strongly when I finished, stood up, and embraced me kindly as he looked at those present, as though in pride. He was only as old as my younger brother Khalid would be today, had my brother Khalid lived. I can see the Leader now, on the First of March, looking at those present with his hand on my shoulder. I imagine he was bidding them farewell, having felt that his end was at hand. Do I merely imagine all this after the passage of these long years? Perhaps, but it is an image that does not leave me as I write these line.

Sa'adah stood up to deliver his traditional speech. I read it again this morning. It is actually the last speech the Leader made, for it is his final document, aside from his "Statement on the First Social Nationalist Revolution," which was distributed when the revolution was declared at the end of June, 1949.

The speech was comprehensive and dealt with issues that he had not treated previously and which, if he had lived longer and followed up, would have perhaps led to basic changes in the Party's ideology and to movement in the direction of socialism. Sa'adah, for the first time, addressed the class issue and attacked the capitalists, characterizing them as "the corrupt class," and he emphasized the rights of the workers and peasants. I don't think Sa'adah was about to adopt the class concept and give up the Social Nationalist concept. He still was far from this position. But he was at the beginning of some radical transformation in his thinking, very much like that which in the 1940s led him to amend the parameters of the Syrian homeland by sanctioning the Fertile Crescent theory. He seemed to want to adopt the social idea along with the nationalist idea as a basis for the Party's doctrine.

The speech, at any rate, was full of new intellectual departures, departures that were some of the deepest things Sa'adah had ever said.

As usual, he uttered his first words in a low voice and in a normal, conversational tone, free from any sharp or angry expression. He recalled the first celebration ever held of the First of March. He mentioned "the hut standing behind a building in Ras Beirut," where that celebration had been held, "the first comrades in the Social Nationalist movement... who carried bouquets of flowers to wish me happy returns on that evening," and the oath he solemnly gave them, "the Party and the whole nation," an oath that was later made an integral part of the Party's constitution.

"I gave the oath," he went on, "not feeling that I was doing the nation a favor. I gave the oath feeling, rather, that I was returning to the nation what belonged to it. All that is in us is from the nation, and all that is in us belongs to the nation. The blood that runs in our veins is not ours: it is only a trust in our custody; and when the nation recalls it, it readily finds it.... Those who live for themselves live within small, limited egos. They seek luxury and personal glory, which they buy with the people's sufferings.... I have said that life for us means a stance of dignity only. I have also said that we kill mere existence in order to establish life.... We want life, not mere existence, and life can only be where there is dignity. As for mere existence, it does not differentiate between itself and humiliation. And how abundant around us is existence with humiliation."

Then he attacked the ruling classes who "do not sympathize with the people's sufferings..., who destroy this nation's sources of life, stand before us to fight with the weapons of vileness and treachery, and annihilate the nation's resources in their evil and mean war." He said that those classes were "our internal Jews" and "that our misfortune with our internal Jews is greater than our affliction with the foreign Jews." He said that a life-and-death conflict between the renaissance and these classes was inevitable. And if the renaissance was not to be victorious, "then decadence will triumph and reaction will conquer...."[15]

I looked at the young faces around me. Failure of the renaissance was not a thought that occurred to anyone. Victory, to them, was inevitable....

What did we want of life? Our families were set against all that we were doing. They always wanted us to leave well enough alone, not to "meddle in politics."

"Beware of politics," every mother would say to her son.

"Leave such matters alone, son," every wise father would say to his son. "Matters of state are not your concern. There are those who take care of them. Your duty is to take care of your future: your studies, earning a degree, obtaining a high-ranking job."

We disobeyed our fathers' orders and deafened our ears to our mothers' entreaties. Unconsciously, we were aiming at the demise of paternal authority, at the rupture of the family siege, and at freedom from our home values. We wanted to replace the individual way of living that we had grown up with in the brackish family circle by a life in the fresh and teeming society at large. We, therefore, took the path of party activity and paid dearly for "our meddling in politics." I speak not only about the [Syrian] Social Nationalists, but also about the Arab Nationalists, the Communists, the Ba'thists, and all those who joined parties and ideological movements that arose in that period.

Where are my friends, my contemporaries, the vanguards of that new generation? Dispersed, and their parties are dismembered. At the forefront was the Syrian Social Nationalist Party, the first to pay the price of revolution. We of that generation are today in our forties and fifties. Our lifetimes are largely behind us now, and our futures have slipped into the past. What was the result of our struggle?

Sometimes I say to myself that it was our fault and that we were the ones responsible for what happened. We could have avoided the misfortunes that befell us. But I think again and say: there was no way out. Our fault was not that we started the revolution, but that we had not sufficiently prepared for it, either in theory or in weapons.

In those days, there was a ghost that accompanied the Leader wherever he went; we sometimes saw him and sometimes not; he was George 'Abd al-Masih. I used to see him at the Leader's home and at the newspaper office whenever I went there. He slept in the sitting room of the Leader's home after the last guest had left, and he got up before sunrise. He wore old clothes and took no care in his appearance. He was the ideal Nationalist, in everyone's opinion. After the Leader was put to death and the Party headquarters moved to Damascus, George 'Abd al-Masih took over the reins and became the Leader's successor and the Party chairman. During his term, the Party was dismembered, and an end was put to it. The fatal blow to it came in 1955 when 'Adnan al-Maliki was assassinated by a bullet shot by a Social Nationalist who was one of George 'Abd al-Masih's faithful "men."

But in my day, that is before the Leader's death, George 'Abd al-Masih wrote next to nothing and had no intellectual pretensions. I remember he wrote a few articles on economics (that had been his field of study at the American University), and they were published in *Al-Jil al-Jadid* under the title "Work: The Nation's Life." His thoughts were unclear and his expression tortuous and difficult. But that did not stop him from writing.

After the Party headquarters moved to Damascus, 'Abd al-Masih began to write daily in the newspaper under assumed names, sometimes several articles per day. He wrote the editorial "Work: The Nation's Life," and other analytical articles. His horizon widened, and he began to write on local politics, international relations, philosophy, and agriculture, as well as economics. He wanted to occupy the place of Sa'adah and be like him in leadership and intellect. In 1954, I lived in Damascus for about a year, while on an academic fellowship. I visited him almost every day. At that time, he suffered from a skin disease on his hands. He sat at his desk—the Leader's desk—and rubbed his hands briskly as he spoke to those gathered about. His habit naturally drew everyone's attention. Someone would soon ask him about his hands, and the conversation would turn to that subject. He said that it was a simple matter: the disease was caused by the paper he wrote on.

How come? Because he wrote continuously for ten hours every day, and his hands were chafed by the rough paper. It was the fault of his abundant writing. Once he said to Sa'id Taqi al-Din in an interview with him in 1953: "I write for about ten hours and read for five. Lecturing and [Party] organization take me several hours more. Some nights I sleep."[16]

I have no doubt now that George 'Abd al-Masih harbored some kind of delusion after he came to occupy the position of Party chairmanship. He wanted to prove to himself and the Party that he was another Sa'adah, hence his explosive flow of continuous writing. His thoughts, however, were just as incomplete, unclear, and odd as they had been before, and they perplexed readers and led to widespread intellectual confusion among the rank and file of the Party. The results of his party politics were more unfortunate and had an even greater adverse effect on the Party. He was the one internally responsible for the divisiveness and the hostility in the Party's legislative and executive councils, especially in the Supreme Council. On the political level, he was responsible for antagonizing the incumbent regime against the Party, despite the fact that Adib al-Shishakli was in power. Notwithstanding all this, his dealings with me were as fine as could be. He always treated me with kindness and affection—perhaps because that was how the Leader had treated me. But let us return here to those few weeks after the celebration of the First of March.

We decided at that time to move the newspaper to a modern press located in al-Jummayza neighborhood and owned by Michel Faddul, a relative of Asad al-Ashqar. (Those who know Beirut will immediately realize that the press was located in the eastern section of the city and in the middle of the area of the Maronite Phalangist Party, the sworn enemy of our Party.) That was our biggest mistake and it indicated my naiveté. I went to the press for the first time on foot from Martyrs' Square, having left the tramway at the Cinema Roxy stop. I crossed Martyrs' Square, passing Abu 'Afif's restaurant, to the intersection of Cinema Empire, then I walked along River Road in the direction of al-Dawra. That was the first time I entered the eastern section of Beirut on foot. I looked at the buildings on both sides of the street, built in the French style of the 1920s and 1930s, and at the contiguous little shops on their ground levels. I felt I was in some city other than Beirut. In fact, when I visited Paris for the first time several years later and saw some of its poorer neighborhoods, I felt I knew the buildings and had seen them previously—and I remembered River Road.

The press was located in a narrow street off River Road. In front of it was a small café. I went up the stairs and entered the first room to the right (the printing machines were on the ground floor). I saw Ra'fat Buhayri bent over at a desk, with his back to the door. The room was virtually empty of furniture, except for the table he was working at and two chairs. When he heard my foot-steps, he turned around. Without greeting me or asking about my health, as was his custom, he said, "The newspaper will never appear today…. Impossible. Everything is missing at the press."

He was angry. Trying to ease his situation, I said, "Of course, everything is missing. Moving is always difficult. Several weeks will pass before we return to our normal routine."

Ra'fat was one of the most famous artists in Lebanon at that time. He was a supporter of the Party and had volunteered to oversee the publication of *Al-Jil al-Jadid* in its new format. My responsibility was to cooperate with him and facilitate his task. We continued to work that evening past midnight until everything was ready and only the printing remained to be done. I said to Ra'fat that I was tired and needed some sleep. He, on the other hand, was in a merry, alert mood. He had drunk *arak* until eleven o'clock, then he ate a dish of hummus and began to drink beer nonstop.

"Go and sleep," he said. "I will stay up until I am sure the printing is going well."

I went downstairs and out into the street, now empty of passersby, and I walked in the direction of Martyrs' Square along a road that passed through the red light district. The road was nearly empty, except for a few drunks asleep on the doorsteps of buildings. I saw faces peering at me from behind the windows of the cheap brothels. The expensive ones were all closed. I passed by Marica, the most famous whorehouse in Beirut, and I remembered my first visit to it in the company of 'Abd al-Latif, Labib, and George Salamah after the graduation ceremony in 1947. In Martyrs' Square, I stood near the police station to wait for a taxi. Within a few minutes, I saw a taxi coming from the direction of Cinema Roxy. I stopped it and got in without bargaining over the fare with the driver. I heard the university clock strike one when I left the taxi in front of the house I lived in. I paid the driver one lira, entered my room, took off my clothes, and went to bed. As usual, I read for a bit until sleep overcame me. I turned off the light and surrendered to a deep sleep, from which I did not wake up until I heard the voice of the newspaper seller calling out: "*Al-Jil al-Jadid. Al-Jil al-Jadid* has appeared." At the beginning, I thought I was dreaming. I opened my eyes and looked at my watch. It was seven o'clock. I jumped out of bed, opened the window, and called at the top of my voice: "Newspapers, newspapers."

I bought five copies for seventy-five piasters. I spread them out on the table and began to examine them. The production was really beautiful. The two colors, red and black, dominated the first page and gave it an attractive strength. The headlines that Ra'fat had chosen were extremely elegant, some written in cursive *ruq'i* hand and others in a large font. Doubtlessly, we had been eminently successful. *Al-Jil al-Jadid* would soon become one of the leading newspapers of Beirut.

I went to the newspaper office in the afternoon. It was a Thursday, June 9. I didn't find Ra'fat in his office, so I asked about him and was told he hadn't come in yet. I sat at my desk and wrote my article for "Our New Life." At about seven o'clock, Ra'fat arrived, his face overflowing with joy.

"What do you think of me?"

And before I answered him, he said, "You haven't seen anything yet. There are things I must examine. The newspaper as it is in my mind has not been realized yet."

"I am satisfied with it as is," I said. "Don't change anything, I beg you. But tell me, where have you been all day? No one has seen you."

"I was at the Saint Simon beach. I slept on the sand all day. I left here at five o'clock, had breakfast at 'Ajami's, then went home, changed my clothes, and returned to the Saint Simon. The newspaper had already gone to the market and the sellers, and they started hawking it. What does the Leader think of it?"

"He liked it very much. I haven't yet seen him today, but I spoke with him by phone."

"By the way. As I was entering just now, I saw people gathering in front of the building. What's happening?"

Speeches and cheers could be heard from across the street. I hadn't noticed anything when I arrived at the press. When I opened the window, we saw a small crowd gathering at the café and at the entrance of the building.

At that moment, the Leader's car arrived. I saw him get out of it, accompanied by 'Ali only. We rushed to receive him. He greeted Ra'fat and thanked him, then he examined the presses and congratulated the workers. He then went upstairs to the office of the editor in chief, and we sat to discuss the contents of the second issue. With us were Faruq Nassar, George 'Atiyyah, and Labib Zuwiyya. After about half an hour, Sa'adah said that he had to return home and asked me to accompany him. As we were getting into the car, I saw young men rushing from the opposite café, gathering at the entrance of the building, and pointing at us. The Leader did not pay attention to what was happening, and the car drove us away without further ado.

Just as we reached the Leader's home, the telephone rang. The Leader picked up the receiver. Wadi' was on the line speaking in a shaking voice and saying that certain Phalangist elements had attacked the newspaper's quarters and shot at the workers on the ground floor, and that the building was besieged. I saw the Leader lower the receiver from his ear, his face sullen; then he raised it again and said, "Get in touch immediately with the police station at Martyrs' Square and ask for help."

Wadi' told him that he had done so already, but that the police hadn't come.

Later we learned the details. The Phalangists had set fire to the ground floor, where the press was. The police arrived, and the officer ordered the Social Nationalists gathered in the upper floor to come down to the street, where he arrested all of them. Among them were George, Faruq, and Labib. As for the Phalangists, the police arrested none of them.

It was evident that the Party was the victim of some prearranged plot of the authorities. In a few hours, the Leader's home was crowded with hundreds of Social Nationalists. The street in front of his house was full of cars and armed men who had come from the suburbs of Beirut and from the Mountain. I went continuously between the house and the street until after midnight. At about one o'clock, I saw the Leader coming down the stairs, and behind him was 'Ali, carrying a brown briefcase. Only those who were in front of the stairs noticed them. I rushed to him and walked next to him as though I was going with him. But he turned to me and said brusquely, "I don't want you to come with me. I'll get in touch with you later."

He turned his back and walked in the direction of the New Oven, which still stands on al-Saydani Street; 'Ali was behind him. Gardens of eggplants and cauliflower still filled that area. The Leader disappeared in the darkness. I suddenly felt exhausted. I looked around and saw the Nationalists gathered in circles here and there. I saw Fu'ad talking enthusiastically in one of the circles. I thought, "The best thing for me is to get some sleep. Tomorrow we'll see what happens."

I walked on Bliss Avenue in the direction of the lighthouse. The street was empty and the darkness dense. When I reached the Shawran descent, I heard sounds of cars coming from a distance. I didn't know that they were laden with policemen who were laying siege to the Leader's home and about to arrest every Social Nationalist they encountered. I entered my room, took off my clothes, read a little, and within minutes was fast asleep.

It was about seven o'clock when I woke up on the morning of Friday, June 11. The weather was wonderful, as it always was in Beirut at that time of the year—that is, at the end of spring and the beginning of summer. A humid breeze blew from the West carrying the smell of the coast, a scent that represents for me the smell of Beirut in the summer, being a mixture of the pungency of seaweed, the warm yeastiness of bagels with sesame seeds, and the tang of humid salt. I left home, not knowing which direction to turn. The Leader was not at his home, the newspaper was closed, and the Party office was undoubtedly being observed. Without thinking, I took the tramway and stood in the rear. Everything appeared to be normal at Bab Idris and al-Ma'rad. I left the tramway in front of the Automatique and crossed the street to the shop of Salim Najjar (Fu'ad's father) near City Hall. His brother Kamal was reading the newspaper *Al-Nahar*. When I entered, my eyes fell on the headlines of the first page: "Burning of the press of *Al-Jil al-Jadid*... Extensive arrests in the ranks of the Nationalist Party in all districts of Lebanon..." I was overcome by a cold dread that I felt at the bottom of my empty stomach. How would I escape, where could I hide when security forces were after me? At that moment, Khalil Khayr Allah entered as though we had had an appointment. In those days, he ran a secondary school in Bhamdun that he himself had established. When he saw me, he stopped in surprise.

"What are you doing here? Don't you know what happened?"

"I've just learned, I read the newspaper."

"You must immediately disappear. There is no fear for Fu'ad, even if he is arrested. As for you, you're one of the responsible persons in the Party. All the responsible persons have been arrested. You are being pursued. Your name has appeared in the newspapers."

"Have they arrested the Leader?"

"It's said they'll arrest him within 24 hours. All roads leading out of Beirut have checkpoints."

"What should I do?"

"Disappear immediately, now."

"How… where?"

Khalil was silent for a moment, then he said, "Come up with me to Bhamdun. It's safest in that village."

I thought for a moment. There was no other place to take refuge. All my friends were arrested now or on the run.

"Let's go."

That decision saved me from sure arrest and imprisonment. Within 48 hours, most of the Social Nationalists in Beirut were arrested; even all those who had any relation whatsoever with the Party were arrested and thrown into prison, either at al-Qal'a or al-Raml. Every day the newspapers published the names of those arrested. But the Leader was still in hiding. So were George 'Abd al-Masih and Fu'ad Shawi (the chief of the Leader's private body-guard).

I hid in Khalil's home in the village of Bhamdun for two days, during which time I did not leave my room. On the third day, Khalil woke me before sunrise, saying that a police force was coming to Bhamdun and that I should leave the house immediately. I quickly put on my clothes, took the book that I had brought with me from Beirut (it was *The Brothers Karamazov*), and the bread and cheese that Khalil gave me, and I followed his younger brother Hafiz. Dawn was breaking behind the mountain, and the air was cold. We walked through the alleys of the village and ascended the mountain path for about an hour before we reached the top. There, I sat under a lone oak tree, propping my back up against its trunk and panting with exhaustion, while Hafiz sat beside me silently. The sun had risen above the mountains, and the snow still covered the high peaks. Hafiz said, "I'll return to the village now. I'll bring you lunch at noon, along with the latest news."

"Don't forget to bring *Al-Hayah* and *Al-Nahar*."

There I was: a fugitive fleeing justice, on the run in the wilderness. What was I doing on top of this mountain? Was what was happening to me real? Or was I dreaming?

Suddenly I heard the roar of propellers and I shook in terror. I saw an airplane high in the sky moving westward. I choked on a lump in my throat. I wished I was in Chicago. I thought of Carol, having earlier forced myself not to think of her. A great sorrow overwhelmed me, and self-pity took possession of me. Tears were about to flow from my eyes, but I said to myself, "Shame on you!"

I controlled myself, ate a small piece of bread and cheese, and soon my morale was up a little. I took Dostoevsky's book and forced myself to read (I still own the very same book).

At noon, I saw Hafiz coming toward me in the distance. His head popped up above the rocks, then disappeared. He was carrying a bundle, which he opened on arriving. It contained grilled *kubbah*, tomatoes, cucumbers, olives, thin flatbread, red cherries, and *Al-Hayah*, the newspaper. He sat down, looking at me as I devoured the food and silently read *Al-Hayah*. Arrests were still being made in all regions. The offices of the Party had been sealed with red wax. A new warrant for the arrest of Antun Sa'adah had been issued (he was still in hiding). The government was accusing the Party of plotting against the state and preparing a coup d'état.

I laid *Al-Hayah* aside and asked Hafiz about the situation in the village.

"There was an extensive surprise search. They searched all the houses but found nothing. They thought that high-ranking Party officials had taken refuge in the village."

"Have the police remained in the village?"

"The commanding officer said they would withdraw in the afternoon."

When Hafiz returned at sunset, he informed me that the police force had withdrawn and that I could return to the house. We returned by the same mountain path. Darkness had fallen on the village square, and most of the inhabitants had gone home, except for a few people playing cards at a small café. Khalil received us at home, laughing and reassured.

"From now on, there is no cause for fear," he said. "You can stay in the house with peace of mind. The soldiers never search the same place twice."

That night I decided not to stay in the village. I felt that I was in a prison of another kind. The villagers could feel the existence of a stranger even if they could not see him. The Party had many enemies in the village, and inevitably another informer's tip would bring the police back. I couldn't sleep and was in a state of constant anxiety.

In the morning of the next day, I told Khalil after an early breakfast that I intended to return to Beirut. He tried to persuade me to stay, but I insisted on leaving. He said, "We must arrange a way for you to enter Beirut."

We agreed that the best way was for me to take a public passenger car from the station, instead of hiring a private car. Khalil accompanied me to the station, where we found a service car about to go. The police stopped us along the way twice, first at the 'Alayh intersection and then at the entrance to Beirut in Furn al-Shubbak. Each time, I showed my student identity card from the University of Chicago. Each time the policeman looked at my innocent face and returned the card to me, no questions asked. We reached Martyrs' Square safely. There, I took the tramway to Ras Beirut. My mother saw me at a distance, walking toward the house. She began to gesture nervously with her hand; I understood she was cautioning me not to go home. I calmly turned around and walked in the direction of the sea, toward the Military Beach. For about an hour, I sat on one of the stone benches that the municipality had built all along the Corniche (most of which were later stolen), then I returned home. When I saw no suspicious signs, I went up the stairs and knocked at the door. My mother opened the door. When she saw me, she said in a trembling voice, "Why have you come back? Don't you know that they are arresting all people, those in the Party as well as others?"

I sat in a seat near the door without saying a word. I drank a glass of lemonade that my maternal aunt offered as she said, "Cool down your blood, sweetheart."

My mother said, "You can't stay here... or in your room. It's impossible."

She was trying to control herself. But her hands were shaking. I regretted having left Bhamdun.

"What do you want me to do?"

In the meantime, my grandmother was reading the Throne verse of the Holy Qur'an [Qur'an 2:255] over my head. Her hands were shaking, too, as she rubbed my hair and pressed my forehead and shoulders. I said to myself: Even the biggest hero would be struck with terror in this atmosphere; run away, man, before you lose your remaining courage. At that very moment, suddenly my mother cried out and made me jump up from my seat in alarm.

"The Pasha's wife.... We'll take you to the Pasha's wife."

It was, in fact, a splendid idea. It would not occur to anyone to look for me at the home of the Pasha's wife. I took a quick shower, put some clothes and books in a small suitcase, and took a taxi with my mother to the home of the Pasha's wife. She lived in a poor street in the Musaytibah neighborhood. The car carried us over a winding road, following my mother's directions, until we reached an old building. Pointing to it, she said, "Stop. This is the house."

We left the taxi, I paid the driver 75 piasters, and we went up a flight of dirty stairs to the third floor. My mother knocked at the door but no one answered. She knocked again with some violence, now beginning to be overcome by anxiety. We heard footsteps approaching the door.

"Who is it?"

"I'm Fatmah, Hanim. I beg you, open quickly."

A lady in her sixties opened the door. She was smoking a cigarette that dangled from her lips. When she saw my mother, she embraced her, saying, "Welcome, welcome to my beloved Fatmah."

The Pasha's wife had changed a lot. Shrunken by age, she was shorter than I remembered and smaller in size. She wore an old dress, longer in the back than in the front. Her chestnut hair had turned gray. We entered the empty sitting room, which had only a small table and three chairs. She and my mother sat down to talk while I stood by the window. My memory took me back to the first time I had seen the Pasha's wife. That was in Jaffa, when I was less than eight years old (we were still living in the Manshiyyah area before moving to the Nuzhah neighborhood). It was a stormy night and my brother Khalid and I had gone to bed. I heard the door being drummed; the lights turned on as the maid rushed to the door. I heard her say, "Who is it?"

Then I heard my mother in the sitting room asking the maid, and the maid answering in a trembling voice, "The Pasha's wife is at the door."

I heard my mother rising quickly and her voice welcoming the important guest. I slipped out of bed stealthily while Khalid remained fast asleep. The door of the reception room was wide open. I saw the Pasha's wife sitting in the place of honor, cross-legged and smoking a cigarette with unaffected pride.

Perhaps in her forties, she was elegantly dressed. Her eyes were green and her legs long. To me, she was gorgeous.

My mother called out to me, "Hanim does not object that you stay a few days at her home."

The Pasha's wife said, "He can stay as long as he wishes. Hisham is most welcome."

It was clear to me that the Pasha's wife had no knowledge of what was happening. I don't think she understood the reason why I was taking refuge with her. I noticed her surprise that I would ask to stay in her house for a few days, but she very likely did not give the matter another thought. All through her life, she gave very little thought to anything. She had lost her wealth without knowing how that had happened, and when she became wretchedly poor, that did not change her attitude to anything.

After my mother left, I sat in the dining room and read *Al-Hayah*, *Al-Nahar*, and the other newspapers I had brought with me. It was Tuesday, June 13. Three days had passed since the beginning of the events. George 'Abd al-Masih was still being pursued. As for the Leader, rumors had it that he was in Damascus, and some said he was hiding in the mountains of al-Shuf. The important thing was that he was still free. *Al-Hayah* mentioned that the government had decided to dissolve the Party, abrogate its legal permit, and bring its leaders to trial.

At sunset, the Pasha's wife entered the room and asked if I was hungry. I said I had no appetite.

She did not say anything more and left the room. She walked about in her little home as though in a dream, smoking one cigarette after another. At night, when I went to bed in a room next to the dining room, I heard her walking to and fro. I was dimly aware of her in this way until dawn. In the fullness of morning, I woke up to the smell of coffee, which she was making on a small electric stove. She gave me a cup and did not ask whether I wanted breakfast. She did not eat anything herself, but continued to smoke her cigarettes and to walk about in her home.

At midday my mother came, bringing a *labanah* sandwich, cherries (my favorite fruit), and *Al-Hayah*. She said that my father had come from 'Amman and that he would have a Jordanian passport issued in my name. She made me a cup of tea, which I drank as I chewed on the *labanah* sandwich and read *Al-Hayah*: it told of arrests of Social Nationalists spreading out, widening, and reaching government circles, the police force, and the army; Sharbil, the prosecutor general, was accusing the Party and claiming that it had planned a coup d'état in Lebanon and was in collusion with Israel.

I said to my mother, "I can no longer stay here. We must find a way for me to leave Lebanon."

She thought a little, then said, "I'll discuss the matter with your father today. I'll return in the afternoon and tell you what happens."

I sat on one of the three chairs in the room and began to follow the movement of the sunshine on the wall. I felt I had been swallowed by some deep desolation. I began remembering the good old days in Chicago and how I had dreamed of returning to Beirut. Here I was in Beirut. Now I longed to return to Chicago.

Before sunset, my mother came and told me that my father had obtained a passport in my name, that a friend of his from a respectable Lebanese family would drive me to Damascus in his car the next day, and that she and my father would cross the border with me.

-9-

We arrived at the Syrian–Lebanese border at sunset on Thursday, June 15. My father was sitting in the front seat beside his friend, the owner of the car, and my mother beside me in the back seat. We passed through Bhamdun, then Sofar, then Dahr al-Baydar. The Biqaʻ plain extended before us with its fertile green fields. Beyond it rose the arid rosy mountain chain, where freedom and safety lay. I looked at the sky, which was as blue as the sea in October, and my heart began to pound. Perhaps my name was on a list at the border police. Perhaps they had a picture of me. In a few minutes, I would become sure of the matter.

In my mind, in the meantime, I saw the policeman approaching the car.

"Please, come out."

"I beg you," screamed my mother. "Have pity, don't take my son."

They paid no attention to her. Chains around my wrists....

The car stopped suddenly. We were at al-Masna', the Lebanese border police station. My father opened the car door and went out, with the four passports in his hand. I saw the soldiers in the distance, talking and smoking and spitting on the ground.

Minutes passed slowly. I turned my face and saw an officer approach, leaning and looking at me inside the car. Looking directly ahead, I held my breath and sat motionless.

"Your name?"

My father said, "This one's passport is stamped with an exit visa."

He gave him my Jordanian passport. The officer looked at it, turned it in his hands, then returned it to my father.

"Okay. Go in peace."

The car drove away. I was still frozen in my seat, still motionless. In a few seconds, we entered Syrian territory. I couldn't believe I was safe. My mother laughed and kissed me. My father turned to me and joked. The nightmare was off my chest all at once, and I felt overwhelmed with joy. I looked around… at the arid land, the rocks, the sky, the stars that had begun to glitter in the twilight, and I swallowed the lump in my throat. I filled my lungs with dry, cold air. Ah!… How beautiful freedom was.

We reached Damascus at about eight o'clock. It was paradise. We stopped at the entrance of the Hamidiyya market and had supper at a little restaurant. My father and I would remain in Damascus overnight in order to travel on to 'Amman in the morning, but my mother returned immediately to Beirut in the company of our family friend.

The first thing that came to my mind in Damascus was Yahya Humsi. His home was located in an old neighborhood near the Saruja market. We found it easily and slept there that night in a room with a high ceiling and locked windows. In the early morning, we took a car to 'Amman and reached it by midday.

-10-

That was my first visit to 'Amman. It was a small city, or rather a large village, crowded with people. The multitudes were, it seemed, all Palestinian refugees. Their camps stretched out in the eastern part of the town on a high mountain and on the hills in the north and to the west. Life in 'Amman was chaotic, and people wandered in the streets, unemployed and aimless. Defeat was depicted on every face and permeated the whole city. People looked as though they had seen ghosts; and their helpless, bewildered eyes said: "We will soon wake up from this dream."

My father and I stayed at my uncle Shakib's home. He was the youngest of my uncles and had lived in 'Amman for many years, exploiting a niggardly plot of arable land near 'Amman that had been in the family for a long time. Uncle Shakib's house was old and had neither running water nor electricity, and the toilet was a hole in the ground outdoors.

On the next day, my father made a reservation for me at a small hotel in midtown, owned by an acquaintance of his from Nablus. At least water and electricity could be had there. I took a bath, changed my clothes, and went out to the street to see if I could find anyone I knew. I don't know how I came across Ishaq Jad Allah, a friend from Jaffa and a former classmate at the Friends' School. I met him by accident, in the street, and I clung to him as a drowning man clings to whatever floats by. Ishaq and I went to the American embassy. I had decided to return, if possible, to Chicago.

The passport officer said that travel visas were not issued in 'Amman, but rather at the American embassy in Damascus. I said,"I would like to have an appointment with the ambassador."

He sent me along to the ambassador's office, but the ambassador's secretary told me that the ambassador did not receive anyone in connection with visas. She added, "If you want to discuss another subject with him, you may come tomorrow at eleven o'clock in the morning."

I said to her, "Yes, I want to discuss another subject with him. Please give me a definite appointment."

I returned the next day in the company of Ishaq. The ambassador received me after a short wait. I had not prepared in my mind what I should tell him. I had thought that as soon as he heard that I was a graduate of the University of Chicago and that I wanted to return to Chicago to continue my studies, he would shake my hand and order someone to give me a visa on the spot.

As soon as I sat down on a chair in front of his huge desk, he asked me, "What can I do for you?"

I told him very politely that I had graduated from the University of Chicago at the beginning of the year with a Master of Arts degree, and that I now wanted to return to complete my studies for the doctorate.

He did not rise to shake my hand as I had expected. Nor did he ring the bell to order me a visa. He looked at me a while in silence, then burst out saying, "You've taken an appointment with me on false pretenses. You want a visa, and the secretary told you that I have nothing to do with visas. This is a diplomatic mission, not a consulate. And yet you've come to ask me for a visa."

He was about to expel me from his office. I did not utter a word. He gazed out the window silently. Then he turned to me and said in a calmer tone of voice, "You should go to our embassy in Damascus. They will give you a visa there."

Instead of thanking him and withdrawing quietly, I asked, "And what documents do I need in order to obtain a visa?"

He glared at me as though he didn't understand what I meant. I repeated my question.

He answered, trying to suppress his anger, "Please, ask the person responsible in the passports department. I am an ambassador here. The office you need is on your left on going out. Please."

He indicated the door with a gesture of his hand. I went out without saying anything. I told Ishaq what happened, then we went to the passport office, and I asked about the documents needed to obtain a visa from Damascus. I spent the rest of the week gathering them and, on Saturday, June 25, I returned to Damascus.

-11-

I did not know when I arrived in Damascus that the Leader had crossed the border into Syria and that he was staying with one of the Social Nationalists near the Orient Hotel. The news about the police crackdowns on the Party had begun to fizzle out and lose its prominence in the newspapers. I thought that a new slumbering period might be beginning in the life of the Party, like the one that transpired after the arrest campaigns of 1938 and 1940, that the Social Nationalists on the run would go underground for a while until matters calmed down and it was possible to reorganize the Party. As soon as I reached al-Marjah Square, I went to the Brazil

Café, where Yahya sat every afternoon. I didn't find him in his usual place, and the waiter explained, "These days, Mr. Yahya prefers the Oasis Café. He may be there."

The Oasis Café, opposite the Brazil Café, was frequented by intellectuals and writers.

I found Yahya sitting there and talking to a young man whom I didn't know. The young man listened to him and, from time to time, puffed his cigarette slowly, seemingly lost in deep thought. Yahya enjoyed listeners of this sort, who listened to him without interruption or argument.

When he saw me, he was astonished. Then he smiled warmly and stood up to embrace me. Our farewells the previous week had been said in the expectation of a long separation. How sweet was the surprise meeting!

I told Yahya what had happened and mentioned to him that I hoped to obtain the American visa as soon as possible, that same day conceivably. He got up at once and called the American embassy, but it was closed and would not open until eight the next morning.

At exactly eight o'clock the next day, Yahya and I were at the door of the consulate attached to the embassy. Three people sat in the waiting room. We waited for about an hour. When my turn came, I entered the consul's office carrying my passport and all the necessary documents and official papers in my hand.

The consul took my passport, examined it, and looked through my documents and official papers. After a while, he raised his head.

"Sorry," he said. "I can't give you a visa. You should go to the American consulate in Cyprus."

I was taken aback by his words. I didn't know whether to laugh or be angry. I said, "The ambassador in 'Amman assured me that you would give me a visa if I had the necessary documents. Here are all the necessary documents. I don't understand what you mean by saying I should go to Cyprus."

"The ambassador in 'Amman didn't know that you had obtained your first visa in 1947 from Jerusalem. We would need your file; now it's at the American consulate in Cyprus."

"But why do you need my old file? You have before you all the documents that I need to obtain a visa. Isn't that so?"

He fell silent for a while, then said, "Let me examine these papers."

The documents were complete. I even had, in place of the original birth certificate, which I couldn't get hold of, a letter that my father and two of his acquaintances had signed and that carried the official seal of a notary public and about twenty revenue stamps of various sizes.

The consul read the English translation of this letter and looked at the signatures and seals in the original document; then he put it aside and said, "There is one document missing."

"Impossible. These are all the documents the ambassador mentioned."

"You need a medical certificate."

He was right. I hadn't remembered that. I rushed with Yahya to a doctor's office, whose address the secretary had given us. He examined me and gave me the required certificate, and we returned to the consulate before closing time.

I presented the certificate to the consul, and he put it in my file with the other documents, saying, "I need six photographs."

I had not forgotten the photographs. In my pocket I had 36 photographs taken in 'Amman, of which I gave him six.

"Come back tomorrow and your visa will be ready at ten o'clock."

We left the consulate happily relieved. Yahya suggested we eat lunch at the Oasis. Instead of taking the bus, we went on foot, despite the heat. At the door of the café, I came face to face with Samir Khuri, who was a Party member and had worked as an architect in Damascus ever since our graduation from the university. It was an exciting and pleasant surprise.

Samir sat with us in one corner of the café and we ordered. He asked why I was in Damascus, and I told him. Yahya rose to greet an acquaintance, so Samir seized the opportunity and whispered in my ear, "Do you know who's in Damascus?"

I immediately knew. "Where is he?"

"I'll take you to him after lunch."

I don't recall how I managed to swallow my food. I said to Yahya that an urgent matter had come up that required that I go with Samir. We agreed to meet that evening.

-12-

I walked silently beside Samir. It was about three o'clock, and the heat was intense. The streets were almost empty. Most shops were closed. Finally, we arrived at a three-story building, which Samir pointed at, saying, "On the second floor."

We went up the stairs, and Samir rang the door bell. We heard heavy footsteps coming toward the door, and a rough voice said, "Who is it?"

"Samir."

A man I didn't know opened the door and led us into the sitting room. I sat there while the man and Samir stood off at some distance, whispering to each other. Then Samir sat beside me and whispered, "The Leader is not here, but he is expected at any moment."

A few minutes later the doorbell rang. The Leader entered with 'Ali behind him and a few other men. When he saw me, he stopped walking and raised his hands in the air, looking surprised and joyful. "You're here? They told me you were arrested."

He embraced me warmly. "Tell me all that happened to you."

I told him in detail what had happened on that ill-omened night. But I did not mention to him why I was in Damascus or anything about my determination to return to Chicago.

He spoke to me about the general state of affairs. He was optimistic and full of vitality and strength. His confidence was contagious.

"There is a task I would like you to do. Can you go to 'Amman tomorrow?"

"By all means. Tomorrow morning."

"Very well. I'll write a letter that you can take to Farid."

It turned out that I had lost touch and had formed no accurate idea about what was happening in the Party. What I thought was a period of stagnation, of dormancy, was, as I was able immediately to gather, a time of rededicated action and preparation. The Party was readying itself for armed revolution in Lebanon.

A handsome, military-looking man in his early thirties opened the door of one of the rooms adjoining the sitting room and entered. The Leader said to him, "This is comrade Hisham. I'd like you to meet him."

He gestured to the military man, saying, "Comrade 'Assaf

Karam, one of our outstanding officers."

As I shook hands with him, I became aware that one of his fingers was missing—amputated? There was some harshness in his smile, as though he might be suffering from severe pain. I learned that he had joined the Party at the end of the 1930s and had been an officer in the French army until the end of the Second World War and that he had participated in the battles on the Egyptian front. For some reason, he had been expelled from the Party during Sa'adah's exile. After the war, 'Assaf Karam was living in Aleppo with his wife and children and was unemployed when the Leader, by fiat, restored his membership rights. It was plainly evident to me that day that 'Assaf Karam had a special standing with the Leader—and enormous influence on him. I now wonder—though I have no way of knowing—what role 'Assaf Karam had played in the Leader's decision to initiate armed revolution in Lebanon after taking refuge in Damascus. The final responsibility, no doubt, was with the Leader, for it was he who decided to go to war, but I believe 'Assaf Karam's arrival in Damascus at that juncture played an important part in the Leader's decision.

That was the last time I heard the Leader speak. He had arrived at the full conviction that the Party was going to be ruined if it did not rise in revolution.

"It is better that we die fighting than preserve an existence that had no life and no dignity."

He said that the feudal alliance ruling Lebanon had decided to put an end to the Party by using all means at its disposal and that there was no longer an opportunity, indeed no justification, for reconciliation or coexistence with the incumbent regime.

"Them or us. Coexistence with them has not been possible. We are a movement that believes in the separation of religion and state and in putting an end to sectarianism and feudalism, and they believe in sectarianism, feudalism, and religious fanaticism. Our existence negates theirs, and their existence negates ours."

He had depended on Husni al-Za'im, who had promised to give the revolution material support; on the Danadishah clan in the Biqa', who announced they were prepared to take part in the revolution; and on Jordan, who had promised to offer weapons, equipment, and ammunition. And none of them had fulfilled their promise. Despite the fact that Sa'adah spoke about the revolution as if its success were assured, in the statement issued on the eve of the revolution he called it "the first Social Nationalist revolution." Did he expect this revolution to fail and to be followed in the future by a second revolution? Did he realize in his innermost being that the revolution was a desperate adventure and that the possibility of its success was extremely limited? I think he did. And yet, he did not show any anxiety. He spoke with confidence and laughed with all his heart as though he had no worry in the world. In my mind, I can see him now, sitting at a table and talking with 'Assaf Karam, studying maps and figures, asking about the minutest details, while 'Assaf Karam answered him with precision and brevity. These two men were planning the destiny of a whole generation. The few coming days would decide whether the Social Nationalist cause would be victorious, or would fail and we return to a life of chaos and humiliation. I was privy to the plan.

The revolution was to break out simultaneously in the various regions of Lebanon. Small groups of Nationalists were to attack the police stations in Beirut, al-Shuf, and al-Matn, and they were to take possession of the largest quantity of arms possible. The revolution would then be declared in al-Harmil, and the force behind 'Assaf Karam, the principal battalion of the revolution, would attack Rashayya and Mashgharah and would occupy the central Biqa' valley. Zero hour was to be at midnight, Saturday, July 2, 1949.

At the appointed time, a group of Social Nationalists attacked the police station of al-Ghubayri in the suburbs of Beirut, and another group attacked the police station of al-Matn in the Mountain. In both incidents, several policemen were injured and the Social Nationalists seized a small quantity of weapons. In al-Shuf and al-Harmil, nothing happened. As for the force of 'Assaf Karam, it entered Lebanese territory in two buses at the appointed time. Sa'adah had accompanied it to the Syrian–Lebanese border, where he had delivered a speech to the Social Nationalists and returned to Damascus. Once in Lebanese territory, the force divided into two groups: the first, under the leadership of 'Assaf Karam, moved toward Mashgharah; and the second, toward Rashayya.

The Lebanese authorities—it came to light later—knew the Party's plan in all its most minute details. As soon as the Nationalists arrived at Mashgharah, they found themselves surrounded.

'Assaf Karam refused to surrender and fought until noon of the next day, when he was killed. The Social Nationalists by his side who were still alive surrendered. The second group was also surrounded at Rashayya—a number of them were killed and the rest surrendered.

On Monday, the last fighting group, under the leadership of George 'Abd al-Masih, was surrounded at Sarhamul in al-Shuf. The fighting did not last long. Some of the fighters surrendered, and the rest were able to escape, including George 'Abd al-Masih.

-13-

Before the failure of the revolution, Sa'adah had asked for a meeting with Husni al-Za'im; and an appointment had been made for him. Now Sa'adah realized that Husni al-Za'im had broken his promise. Sa'adah had two choices: either to meet with Husni al-Za'im or to escape and seek refuge in Jordan.

In the company of Samir Khuri, he got into Subhi Farhat's car and ordered Subhi to drive southward. Samir told me the details of the trip. He said that the Leader did not utter a word until the car reached the outskirts of Dir'a, then said to Subhi, "Return to Damascus."

He decided en route that his escape would benefit no one. He resolved to take a last risk. When the car neared Damascus, he asked Subhi to drive to the president's palace. Just before the car reached the palace, Sa'adah asked Samir to leave and kindly bade him farewell.

As soon as the car entered the outer courtyard of the palace, a group of soldiers surrounded it and apprehended Sa'adah (Subhi Farhat was also arrested and sent to al-Mazzah prison). They put the Leader in an army car that took him to the Syrian–Lebanese border, where Farid Shihab, the Lebanese public security director, and Nur al-Din al-Rifa'i, chief of the police, were waiting for him. These officials took him to Beirut in handcuffs.

-14-

I, too, had had a role. At six o'clock on our last day together, the Leader gave me the letter that I was to take to 'Amman.

"Emphasize to Farid that this is urgent. Any delay will harm us very much."

"What should I do after delivering the letter?"

"Return to Damascus. I need you here." He smiled, put his hand on my shoulder, and said, "You don't know how to fight, but you can help in other ways. I want you here beside me."

At half past six, I said goodbye to him. I was confident that I would see him in a few days, and that the revolution would be victorious.

I walked in the street, whistling merrily and looking at the passersby and the shops. My heart was overflowing with joy. When I met Yahya, he hastened to ask me, "Good news, I hope. It seems you're happy. What's up?"

I told him that I had met a very dear friend of mine and that I was leaving for 'Amman the next morning. He suggested that we go to the cinema, so I agreed enthusiastically. We saw an American movie, then went to the Oasis for beer and did not go home until one o'clock. I slept soundly and had pleasant dreams, all of which I forgot when I woke up.

-15-

I arrived in 'Amman at about noon. I got in touch with Farid and gave him the letter and conveyed to him what the Leader had said about the importance of quick action. I told him that I would return to Damascus the next day, but he asked me to delay my departure to the day after that, i.e., Saturday. So I agreed.

I spent Friday alone, walking the streets of 'Amman. Ishaq was busy that day; he had begun work at the American embassy. At noon, I found myself near the old mosque in Wadi 'Amman. The street was full of people as prayer time was approaching. Suddenly I saw motorcycles and police cars coming toward the mosque, and behind them was King 'Abdallah's car, followed by jeeps full of soldiers. The police cars stopped in front of the mosque, and dozens of policemen jumped out of them, carrying canes in their hands. They beat the people who stood at the entrance of the mosque and shouted: "Clear the way, clear the way." I heard a cane tear the air near me as it fell on the head of a man standing beside me. The man, wearing a *kufiyya* and rope, raised his hand to his face, and I saw blood flowing from his head. The policeman who had dealt him the blow shouted at him, "Be gone, you dog."

The policeman was hitting indiscriminately with his cane, right and left, and people ran before him like mice. I saw the religious elders and the notables rush to receive the king, bowing and kissing his hand. He was wearing a white cloak and a turban-like headdress. I thought I was in a dream, in another time and place.

On the next day, I returned to Damascus. From the moment we entered the city, I felt that there was something extraordinary in the atmosphere. I left the car and walked toward Yahya's home. Before I entered the Sarujah market, I saw George Salamah, Joseph's brother. He told me that he had been able to escape from Beirut and was in a state of great anxiety. He said, "You should return to 'Amman immediately. Everyone in Syria is being pursued."

I asked him about the Leader, and he said that the Leader had disappeared and nobody knew where he was.

Once again, I was seized by that sweeping fear that I had experienced in Beirut, and I felt cold blood flowing in my veins. We were now being pursued in Syria as we had been and still continued to be in Lebanon. Thus, in the wink of an eye, Damascus was changed from a friendly, safe place into a terrifying, dangerous one—like Beirut.

I rushed to Yahya's house but didn't find him there. I went to the Oasis Café. I found him sitting alone, reading a newspaper. As soon as he saw me, he blurted out, "What are you doing here? Why have you returned from 'Amman? Haven't you heard the news?"

He then told me about the rumors that had begun to spread in Damascus: that Adib al-Shishakli had been dismissed or transferred from his office, that Husni al-Za'im had handed Sa'adah over to the Lebanese government, and that al-Mazzah prison was full of arrested people. I sat on a chair and felt terribly exhausted and extremely hungry. Then Yahya and I went to a little restaurant across the street from the Socrates Restaurant; we ate a bread soup with sheep shanks, and my morale rose a little. Yahya said, as we drank the coffee, "The important thing is to arrange for your trip back to 'Amman. The first thing we must obtain is an exit visa from Public Security."

"I don't think that they have lists of Nationalists coming from

Lebanon."

"Unless they obtained them through the Lebanese Public Security. At any rate, I'll go with you to Public Security so that, if anything happens, we will at least know."

I didn't sleep that night until dawn, when I dozed off for an hour or so. It was Sunday, July 3. Yahya and I left the house at seven o'clock. We had a cup of tea at a little café in front of Public Security as we waited for the offices to open. At half past seven, we entered the Public Security building. I was surrendering to fate and felt a sort of reassurance. A few people were waiting in one of the corners of the visa office while the employees drank coffee and read the papers. I approached the window labeled "Exit Visas," and I placed my passport in front of the employee. He was reading the newspaper and paid no attention to me, so I said, "Good morning. Please, do me the favor…"

I pushed my passport toward him. He looked at me with some annoyance, put the newspaper aside, and examined the passport. He then opened a dossier and moved his eyes back and forth between it and the passport as if comparing my name with other names. I saw him take a pencil and write something in the dossier. And before I knew what was happening, he pushed the passport toward me stamped with an exit visa and went back to read his newspaper.

I went out quickly to where Yahya was waiting for me in front of the entrance. His face expressed his relief on seeing me.

"We can catch the eight o'clock service car, if we hurry."

The station of the 'Amman service cars was not very far from the Public Security building; we reached it in a few minutes. We found an empty seat in a car about to go. Yahya stood by the car, still worried, and wanted the car to take off. When the driver turned on the engine, Yahya stretched out his hand to shake mine and said, "I don't want to see you for a long while."

Then he put his hand on the back of my head tenderly. That was the last time I saw him.

We were delayed on the border for an inspection and did not reach 'Amman until mid-afternoon. I went directly to the hotel, took a cold bath, then slept fitfully through the night. In the morning, I went down to the street and bought the newspapers. I read the news of the defeat, of 'Assaf Karam's death, and the surrender of the Social Nationalists in the Biqa'.

Although I had expected bad news, I was shocked by what happened. The Party was utterly ruined. The government could now clearly accuse us of rebellion and revolution. Until now, the Party had seemed innocent in people's eyes, for the accusation of planning a coup d'état had been just talk. But now the situation had changed drastically.

What could I do? I waited for Ishaq to finish his workday, and together went to al-Zarqa' and sat at a café over coffee, listening to the news on the radio: new arrests in Lebanon, widespread arrests in Syria, details of the battles of the Biqa' and the Matn. People around us at the café were paying no attention, as though what was happening was taking place in China. For whose sake, I wondered, are we suffering and sacrificing? Our society, I thought, was cruel and merciless. Worst of all, it had no mercy for its own sons. He who raised his head was beaten, disdained, and fed earth. My homeland, how unfortunate you are.

I was licking my wounds, feeling alone, at the café of al-Zarqa', having forgotten my brethren in struggle—the Communists, the Arab Nationalists, the socialist Ba'thists, the Muslim Brothers— who were all on the same road. All we had, we had given to these people and to this nation, each in his own way. They always took from us all that was worth anything, and then they threw us in prison and accused us of treason. Antun Sa'adah and his Party were the first new victims.

-16-

On Friday morning, July 8, when I went out of the hotel, the first thing I heard was the newspaper seller shouting: "The execution of Antun Sa'adah in Lebanon."

I went through a mechanical set of motions to buy the news-paper and walked to the bus station. I felt that things around me had shut down. Complete silence reigned over everything. People were walking, but it was like a silent movie. The sounds of the external world were not reaching me; they were turned off as one turns off a radio or a light. I heard something resembling a roar coming from a distance. I felt dizzy. Once, many years ago, I had fallen on the ground on the football field at the Friends' School; my head had hit a rock and I was carried away unconscious. Before becoming unconscious, I had experienced this same sensation of complete silence and I heard the same roar coming from a distance. It was a kind of death.

I got hold of the bus door, boarded, and sat in the first empty seat I saw. I opened the newspaper. A picture of Sa'adah before the military court in Beirut appeared prominently on the front page. He wore his beige summer suit, a suit he had brought with him from Argentina. He was unshaven and looked tired in spite of the defiant look on his face. He was surrounded by soldiers but did not look like a captive. This was the end of the line. He must have realized that. I knew what was going on in his head: he wanted to say his last words and leave with an uplifted head. It was the final stance of dignity.

Words of his come to my mind: "I must forget my own bleeding wounds in order to help bandage the severe wounds of my nation." He had been a young man in his early twenties, in Brazil, when he inscribed those words in his diary.

I can now hear his voice speaking out in the last celebration of the First of March: "All that is in us is from the nation, and all that is in us belongs to the nation. The blood that runs in our veins is not ours: it is only a trust in our custody, and when the nation recalls it, it readily finds it."

His words over the years: "We kill mere existence in order to establish life.... Be heroic and don't be afraid of war, be rather afraid of failure.... We shall change the face of history.... Life is a stance of dignity..."

—Five—

-1-

The details of the tragedy were published on the next day (Saturday, July 9, 1949).

Sa'adah had been handed over by the Syrian Public Security to the Lebanese authorities on Tuesday, July 5, and was taken under guard to al-Shayyah, where he was held in the room of the commanding police officer until early in the morning of Wednesday, July 6; then he was moved to the military court.

The military court consisted of: Lieutenant Colonel Anwar Karam as chairman, and Captains Samrani and Ahdab, Lieutenant 'Arab, and Mr. Ghibriyal Basila at the bench. The prosecutor general was Yusuf Sharbil. When the court refused the request of the defense attorney to delay the trial for 24 hours so that he could have an opportunity to study the case and prepare his defense, that attorney resigned, and the court replaced him with an officer from the army. Sa'adah spoke in his own defense, but journalists were not allowed in the courtroom and his defense was not published.

At half past seven in the evening, the court issued its sentence, which was execution by firing squad. The cabinet headed by Prime Minister Riyad al-Sulh issued a decree approving the sentence, and it was immediately signed by Bisharah al-Khuri, president of the republic.

At half past eight, the Leader was transferred from the military court to al-Raml prison, where he was placed in solitary confinement.

Al-Nahar reported what happened in the last few hours, as filed by a correspondent who had been permitted to enter the prison and meet with the Leader.

> ... Sa'adah had no knowledge that the sentence had been approved. As soon as he entered into solitary confinement, he took off his jacket, undid his necktie, lay down on the bed, and slept for the first time in more than 24 hours....
>
> He woke up, sat on the bed, looked around him, and understood but did not say a word.
>
> The prosecutor general came, conveyed to him the fact that the pardon committee had endorsed the sentence, as had His Excellency the president of the republic. When he began to read the approval decree,

Sa'adah said to him, "Enough, enough."

He was asked whether he needed food or coffee. He said a cup of coffee would be sufficient. He was offered a cigarette, but he said he did not smoke much.

As he was calmly drinking the coffee, he looked at the judges and asked them in a serious tone, speaking in classical Arabic as was his custom: "What law in any country in the world permits a death sentence before the passage of at least 48 hours after it is issued?"

No one answered him.

Then he asked whether he would be allowed to see his wife and three daughters. He was told no. At that moment, a tear appeared in his eye and he was overcome by emotion. But he shook his head and smiled with visible bitterness.

When the prosecutor general asked him to write his will, he said he willed that his property in Duhur al-Shuwayr be divided equally among his wife and daughters, so that each one of them would have a quarter. He willed that the money he had on him amounting to 400 liras be given to his wife, and he also willed to her the furniture of his home. Then he asked whether the law permitted him to appoint his wife as guardian of his children. He was told that such matters remained within the jurisdiction of the civil law court but, at any rate, he could write his wish in the will, so he did.

Then he asked to be allowed to make a political statement, but he was told that there were no journalists present and that there was no use in a statement anyhow. He responded by saying that he wished to record a statement for history, even though they were only minutes from implementing the sentence. He was allowed, so he said:

"I believe that the Lebanese government has widely conspired against me and my Party, but I look with contempt at those who conspired against me and those who sentenced me to death and those who will execute me." [Al-Nahar, 9 July 1949]

The death sentence was carried out in the early hours of dawn near the seashore in the firing range at Bir Hasan. His body was carried to St. Elias church at nearby Tina, where the priest prayed over it in the presence of soldiers who had shot him. Then the body was interred in the church burial ground.

-2-

The airplane rises little by little above 'Amman and moves southward. The houses become so small that they appear like children's toys. Then they disappear. Only the empty land and arid hills remain. I look at them through tears that I cannot keep from flowing.

My homeland, you have spurned me.... I shall never return to you.... I shall never ever return to you....[17]

Notes

1 The full text of the speech is in *Al-Nizam al-Jadid* [The new order] (Damascus, 1950): 102–106.

2 In India.

3 "The Leader's Letter to Lloyd George," *Al-Nizam al-Jadid* (January 1950): 25–36.

4 "Memorandum of the Syrian Nationalist Party to the League of Nations and the United Nations," *Al-Nizam al-Jadid* (January 1950): 44.

5 Ibid.

6 "The Leader's Communiqué Regarding the Partition of Palestine," *Al-Nizam al-Jadid* (January 1950): 48.

7 A letter from the Leader to Hisham Sharabi, June 23, 1949.

8 "Paragraphs from the Leader's speech in Jizzin on October 15, 1948," *Al-Nizam al-Jadid* (December 1950): 50–51.

9 Ibid., 56.

10 Ibid., 58.

11 Wahl did not like this expression and crossed it out.

12 Friedrich Nietzsche, *Thus Spake Zarathustra*, first part, discourse VIII.

13 "Sections from Sa'adah's Speech in Ras Beirut on the Occasion of the First of March 1949," *Al-Nizam al-Jadid* (June 1950): 111–113.

14 "The Leader's Speech on the First of March, 1943," *Al-Nizam al-Jadid* (June 1950): 91.

15 "Sa'adah's Speech on the First of March, 1949," *Al-Nizam al-Jadid* (June 1950): 114–118.

16 Sa'id Taqi al-Din, *Al-Kitabat al-Kamila* (Beirut, 1965): 78–90.

17 After his retirement from Georgetown University in 1998, Professor Hisham Sharabi returned to live in Lebanon and died in Beirut on Thursday, January 13, 2005. [Trans.]